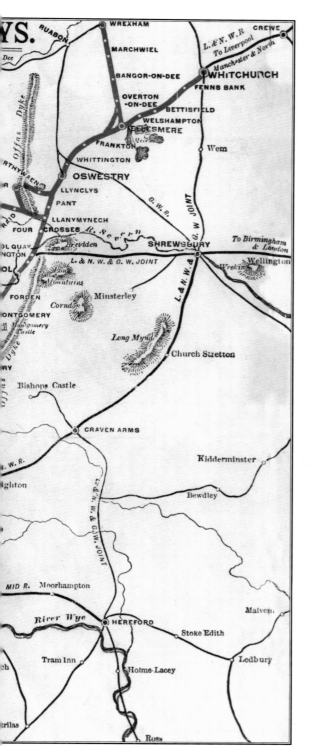

Th... to
the Ca... ed
and bea... y,
to whic... rs
great... of
firm, sa... in
its pu... of
SNOW... he
BEACONS, with their Rivers and Lakes, are also readily accessible from the various Watering-places, thus placing within the reach of visitors a delightful combination of the natural beauties of sea and land. The Upper Valleys of the Wye, the Severn, and the Usk, through which the Line runs to Brecon, also possess great attractions to Tourists and Anglers. A special feature are the magnificent Coach Drives, particulars of which are given in the Rail and Coach Tour Programme (issued July) to be had gratis at all Cambrian Stations. The following are some of the Principal Places of interest in the neighbourhood of Stations on the Coast Section of the **CAMBRIAN RAILWAYS.**

STATION.	NAME OF PLACE.
ABERYSTWYTH	Castle Ruins, University College, Rocks and Caves, Llanbadarn Church, Devil's Bridge, Ponterwyd, Plynlimon, Rheidol Lake. Excellent bathing. Promenade Pier and Cliff Railway.
BORTH	Sands, Cliffs, Taliesin. Golf and bathing.
GLANDOVEY...	Llyfnant Valley, Glaspwll Cascade, Cwmrhaiadr Waterfall.
MACHYNLLETH	Miniature Gauge Railway, Corris Slate Quarries, Cader Idris, Talyllyn Lake.
ABERDOVEY...	Dovey Estuary and Harbour. Golf and bathing.
TOWYN	Miniature Gauge Railway, Abergynolwyn Slate Quarries, Cader Idris, Talyllyn Lake, Bird Rock, and Happy Valley. Magnificent promenade and good bathing.
ARTHOG	Waterfalls, Cader Idris.
PENMAENPOOL	Cymmer Abbey, Gold Mines.
DOLGELLEY	Precipice Walk, Torrent Walk, Tyn-y-groes, Cader Idris, Gold Mines.
BARMOUTH	Mawddach Estuary, Viaduct*, Panorama View, Llanaber Church. Good sea-bathing and golf.
DYFFRYN	Cromlechs, Cors-y-Gedol Lakes.
LLANBEDR AND PENSARN	Mochras Island Glenatro, Cwm-Bychan Lake, Drws-Ardudwy, Rhinog Valley.
HARLECH	Castle, Sands, Golf, and good sea-bathing.
PENRHYNDEUDRAETH ...	Vale of Festiniog, Tan-y-bwlch, and Maentwrog (by road).
MINFFORDD	Miniature Gauge Railway, Festiniog Slate Quarries, Tan-y-bwlch, and Maentwrog (by rail).
PORTMADOC...	Traethmawr, Pass of Aber-Glaslyn, Beddgelert, Snowdon, Gwynant Lake.
CRICCIETH	Castle, Druidical Circles. Excellent bathing.
PWLLHELI	Gimlet Rock, Porth Dinlleyn, Lleyn Peninsula, the Rivals, Excellent bathing. Nevin, Abersoch, Clynnog, Llanbedrog, & Glynyweddw Mansion.

CHEAP DAY TICKETS are issued between above Stations, June to October inclusive.
* Weekly Tickets for foot passengers on Barmouth Viaduct, Price 6d.
Compartments reserved and Special Through Carriages provided for Families and Parties on application.
New Corridor Carriages lighted with gas.
Vehicles run between Pwllheli and Nevin in connection with the Cambrian Trains.
Time-tables, showing the communication between Stations on the Cambrian Railways and all parts of the Country, Tourist Programmes, and further particulars of Trains, Through Carriages, Fares, &c., may be obtained at any of the Company's Stations or Booking Offices, or on application to Mr. W. H. GOUGH, Superintendent of the Line, Oswestry, and from the undersigned.

C. S. DENNISS, *Secretary & General Manager.*
General Offices, Oswestry.

The Cambrian Railways

Portrait of a Welsh Railway Network

The
Cambrian Railways
Portrait of a Welsh Railway Network

REX CHRISTIANSEN

Ian Allan
PUBLISHING

Half title:
Summer on the coast line in 1956: a Machynlleth-Pwllheli stopping train departs from Minffordd, past the Festiniog Railway exchange sidings. Minffordd ground frame is housed in the platform cabin. A GWR 2-6-2T heads a rake of corridor coaches. *R. E. Vincent*

Title page:
The Mid-Wales Railway was noted for its isolated junctions: Moat Lane, Builth Road, Three Cocks, seen here, and Talyllyn. In the final years before closure, just ahead of the 1963 Beeching Report, small Standard Moguls had taken over trains from a host of veteran locomotives. In summer 1959, No 46513 heads the 12.30pm Builth Road-Brecon (left), which connected at Three Cocks with the 12.42pm from Hereford, which terminated there. It had arrived behind No 46519. *R. Tuck*

Front cover: The 2.43pm up stopping train is dwarfed by the historic castle as it departs from Harlech on 15 July 1911. It is headed by 'Beaconsfield' class 4-4-0 No 50, dating from 1891. *From a painting by George Heiron, based on a photograph in the R. W. Miller collection*

Back cover: Former Cambrian Railways 0-6-0 No 892 leaves Harlech in February 1941. *Colour-Rail (GW22)*

First published 1999

ISBN 0 7110 2691 2

© Ian Allan Publishing Ltd 1999

Published by Ian Allan Publishing

an imprint of Ian Allan Publishing Ltd, Terminal House, Shepperton, Surrey TW17 8AS.

Printed by Ian Allan Printing Ltd, Riverdene Business Park, Hersham, Surrey KT12 4RG.

Code: 9910/B1

Bibliography

Selective because there are so many books about the Cambrian Railways and other railways of north and mid-Wales.

Baughan, P. E.;	*Regional History of Railways: North and Mid Wales*
Boyd, J. I. C.;	*Narrow Gauge Railways in Mid Wales*
Boyd, J. I. C.;	*Narrow Gauge Railways in South Caernarvonshire*
Briwnant-Jones, G.;	*Railway Through Talerddig*
Cartwright, R. and Russell, R. T.;	*The Welshpool & Llanfair Light Railway*
Christiansen, R. and Miller, R. W.;	*The Cambrian Railways* (2 volumes)
Christiansen, R.;	*Forgotten Railways: North & Mid Wales*
Cozens, L.;	*The Llanfyllin Railway*
Cozens, L.;	*The Mawddwy Railway*
Cozens, L.;	*The Van and Kerry Railways*
Dalton, T. P.;	*Cambrian Companionship*
Gasquoine, C. P.;	*The Story of the Cambrian*
Green, C. C.;	*Cambrian Railways 1859-1947*
Green, C. C.;	*The Cambrian Coast Lines* (2 vols)
Jones, E. V.;	*Mishaps on the Cambrian Railways*
Johnson, P.;	*The Cambrian Lines*
Kidner, R. W.;	*The Cambrian Railways*
Kidner, R. W.;	*The Mid Wales Railway*
Lewthwaite, G. C.;	*Branch Line Index*
Rear, W. G. and Williams, M. F.;	*The Cambrian Coast Railway*
Wren, W. J.;	*The Tanat Valley: Its Railways and Industrial Archaeology*

Also consulted:

Cambrian Railways board minutes at BRB Historical Records, the *Railway Magazine* and journals and magazines of the Branch Line Society, Manchester Locomotive Society, Railway & Canal Historical Society, Railway Correspondence & Travel Society, Railway Ramblers, Wirral Railway Circle, *Bradshaw's* Shareholders' Guides and Timetables, timetables of the Cambrian Railways, London & North Western, Great Central and Great Western Railways and Cambrian-associated standard and narrow gauge railways.

Contents

Picture credits
Line illustrations, maps and reproduced posters etc are not credited; all are from the Author's Collection. Photographic material from large collections is credited: *IAL* — Ian Allan Library; *LCGB* — Locomotive Club of Great Britain; *LGRP* — Locomotive & General Railway Photographs; *LPC* — Locomotive Publishing Club; *SLS* — Stephenson Locomotive Society.

Note: place names
During the existence of the Cambrian Railways, many larger Welsh towns were known by anglicised spellings of their names. This convention is followed in this book for historical reasons, although long obsolete in Wales.

Acknowledgements
This portrait has been sharpened and enlivened by information and memories of a number of people who wrote after the two-volume history by R. W. (Bob) Miller and myself was published some three decades ago. Among them were Jeffrey Williams, Dr W. J. Wren and Oliver Veltom, who saved the Vale of Rheidol from closure in the BR era. Through the years I have valued the help of Bob Miller, who has read the manuscript, Gordon Biddle, Harold Forster MBE, Nigel Payton, Richard Price and fellow members of the Railway & Canal Historical Society.

     This book was written at the behest of Peter Waller, publishing manager, Ian Allan Publishing, who has once again demonstrated a refreshing approach to queries.

Rex Christiansen
Chelford, Cheshire 1999

MAIN LINE.—Whitchurch and Aberystwyth.

Miles.	DOWN.	WEEK DAYS. H am	am Tuesdays only. Third Class only. On Newtown Fair days 55 mins. earlier.	am	am	am	H am	am	H pm NORTH EXPRESS	H pm LONDON EXPRESS.	H pm	H pm	pm	pm LONDON EXPRESS.	pm	pm Mondays only. Third Class only.	pm Wednesdays only	pm	pm	pm	SUN. am
—	**WHITCHURCH** ... ...dep	2 25		...	...	8 20	10 7	1015	1217	...	...	1 50	2 0	...	...	...		5 20	6 40	8 42	2 25
3	Fenn's Bank ... ... ,,	*		...	...	8 27	C	1023	...	...	...	...	2 7	...	...	...		5 28	6 48	8 49	*
6¾	Bettisfield ... ... ,,	*		...	...	8 34	C	1031	...	...	...	...	2 20	...	...	...		5 36	6 56	8 56	*
8	Welshampton ... ... ,,	*		...	...	8 37	..	1035	...	...	...	...	2 24	...	...	...		*	7 0	9 0	*
11	**Ellesmere** ... ... ,,	2 55		...	...	8 55	10 29	1045	1235		...	2 13	2 31		...	...		5 50	7 9	9 8	2 55
13	Frankton ... ... ,,	*		...	...	9 0	...	1050	...		...	...	2 36		...	...		5 55	7 14	9 13	*
16¼	Whittington ... ... ,,	*		...	...	9 8	C	1058	...		...	...	2 44		...	...		6 1	7 23	9 23	*
18¼	**OSWESTRY** ... arr	3 15		...	...	9 13	10 43	11 3	1247		...	2 28	2 48		...			6 6	7 28	9 28	3 15
	dep	3 25		...	8 5		10 48		1250		...	2 35	2 53		3 45		5 0	6 12	7 35		6 15
22	Llynclys ... ... ,,	...		...	8 13	...	10 56	...			...	...	3 0		3 55		5 10	6 20	7 45	...	6 23
23¼	Pant ... ... ,,	...		...	*	...	...	...			...	...	3 3		3 59		5 13	*	7 50	...	...
24¼	Llanymynech ... ...arr	*		...	8 18	...	11 0	...			...	...	3 6		4 3		5 17	6 24	7 54	...	6 29
33¼	**Llanfyllin** ... dep	...		...	7 30	...	10 15	...			...	...	1 45		...		...	5 55	7 20	...	...
	arr	...		...	8 55	...	11 35	...			...	...	...		4 35		...	7 0	8 30	...	...
24¼	Llanymynech ... ...dep	*		...	8 20	...	11 1	.			...	...	3 8		...		5 20	6 27	7 57	...	6 30
25¾	Four Crosses ... ... ,,	...		...	8 25	...	11 5	...			...	...	3 12		...		5 25	6 32	8 1	...	6 35
27½	Arddleen ... ... ,,	...		..	Mon	...	...	...			...	...	Wed		...		5 31	...	...	...	...
29¼	Pool Quay... ... ,,	*		...	8 35	...	11 13	...			...	...	3 20		...		5 37	6 39	8 11	...	6 42
31¼	Buttington ... ... ,,	*		...	8 40	...	11 17	...			...	...	3 25		...		5 42	6 47	8 16	...	6 48
34	**WELSHPOOL** ... arr	3 55		...	8 45	...	11 22	...	1 12		...	3 3	3 30		pm		5 50	6 52	8 22	...	6 54
	dep	4 12	7 55	...	8 50	...	11 30	...	1 14	2 15	...	3 10		3 35	4 20	5 30		7 10	8 28	...	7 0
38½	Forden ... ... ,,	...	8 5	...	9 0	...	D	...	...	...	...	...	...	...	4 28	5 40		7 18	8 36	...	7 9
40¼	Montgomery ... ... ,,	4 24	8 10	...	9 4	...	11 41	...	1 25	O	...	B	...	B	4 32	5 50		7 23	8 45	...	7 13
44	Abermule ... ... ,,	...	8 20	..	9 11	...	*	...	...	...	...	...	...	...	4 42	6 0		7 30	8 53	...	7 20
47½	Kerry ... dep	...	...	...	8 40	...	11 20	...	...	...	...	...	...	...	3 50	...		7 0	...	...	...
	arr	...	...	...	10 5	...	12 25	...	...	...	...	...	...	...	5 10	...		...	9 20	...	...
47¾	**NEWTOWN** ... ...dep	4 41	8 30	...	9 25	...	12 0	...	1 42	O	...	3 40	...	4 5	4 54	6 10	Wednesday only	7 46	9 6	...	7 34
52¼	**Moat Lane Junction** arr	4 49	Tuesdays only.	...	9 33	...	12 8	...	1 50	2 50	...	3 48	...	4 18	5 2			7 54	9 15	...	7 43
	dep	4 55		...	9 38	...	12 12	...	1 55	2 52	3 35	3 54	...	4 23	5 7			8 6		...	7 48
53½	Caersws ... ... ,,	4 58		...	9 42	...	D	...	...	...	...	...	...	...	5 10			*	...	...	7 51
55	Pontdolgoch ... ... ,,	...		...	*	...	...	...	...	...	...	...	...	...	*			...	...	...	7 54
59¼	Carno ... ... ,,	5 11		...	9 52	...	D	...	...	...	...	...	...	...	5 23			A	...	...	8 2
61¼	Talerddig ... ... ,,	...		...	*	...	...	...	...	...	...	...	...	...	*			...	...	...	...
64¾	Llanbrynmair ... ... ,,	5 20		...	10 2	...	D	...	...	...	...	...	...	...	5 35			A	...	...	8 16
70	Cemmes Road ... ... ,,	5 29		...	1014	...	12 52	...	...	...	4 10	B	...	B	5 43			8 41	...	...	8 30
75	**Machynlleth** ... arr	5 37	am	...	1023	pm	1 0	...	2 43	3 32	4 18	4 38	...	5 2	5 52		pm	8 50	...	...	8 40
	dep	5 42	8 35	9 45	1028	1220	1 10	...	2 47	3 35	4 20	4 41	...	5 5	5 55		6 55	8 55	...	...	8 45
79	**Dovey Junction** ... arr	...	8 43	9 52	1035	1230	1 18	...	2 55	...	4 27	4 48	...	5 12	...		7 3	..	...	...	...
	dep	...	8 48	1010	1043	1255	1 28	...	2 57	...	4 32	4 51	...	5 17			7 10	...	...	...	...
79¾	Glandyfi ... ... ,,	5 50	8 51	1013	D A	1259	B B	...	B	...	4 34	...	...	...	6 3		7 13	A	...	...	8 54
85¼	Ynyslas ... ... ,,	...	9 3	1024	D A	1 10	B B	...	B	...	...	...	...	...	6 14		7 25	...	...	...	9 6
87¼	Borth... ... ,,	6 2	9 7	1029	11 3	1 20	1 50	...	B	B B	4 48	B	...	B B	6 20	...	7 30	9 18	...	...	9 10
89¾	Llanfihangel ... ... ,,	...	9 12	1036	D A	1 25	B B	...	...	...	O O	...	...	...	W	...	7 36	...	...	...	9 16
91¼	Bow Street ... ... ,,	6 11	9 20	1041	D A	1 30	B B	...	...	...	5 0	...	...	...	6 35	...	7 41	A	...	...	9 23
95¾	**ABERYSTWYTH** ... ...arr	6 20	9 30	1050	1125	1 40	2 10	...	3 35	4 20	5 10	5 20	...	5 45	6 45	...	7 55	9 35	...	...	9 35

Wrexham, Ellesmere, etc.

[No Sunday Trains.]

Miles.	DOWN.	WEEK DAYS. am	am	am	pm	pm	pm	pm
—	**WREXHAM (Central)**...dep	8 15	9 50	11 55	1 35	4 0	6 35	8 30
2¼	Marchwiel... ... ,,	8 20	9 55	12 0	1 40	4 5	6 40	8 35
5¼	Bangor-on-Dee ... ... ,,	8 28	10 3	12 8	1 46	4 13	6 48	8 43
8½	Overton-on-Dee ... ... ,,	8 35	1010	12 15	1 52	4 20	6 55	8 50
12¾	**Ellesmere** ... ...arr	8 45	1020	12 25	2 0	4 30	7 5	9 0
	Whitchurch ... ...arr	9 25	1212	12 55	2 35	5 10	...	1025
	Oswestry ... ... ,,	9 13	1043	12 47	2 28	6 6	7 28	9 28

Miles.	UP.	WEEK DAYS. am	am	pm	pm	pm	pm	pm
	Oswestry ....dep.	8 35	1125	1 50	3 2	5 25	...	...
	Whitchurch .... ,,	8 20	1015	1 50	2 0	5 20	6 40	8 42
—	**Ellesmere** ....dep.	9 5	1150	2 20	3 30	5 55	7 15	9 15
4¼	Overton-on-Dee .... ,,	9 15	12 0	2 30	3 40	6 5	7 25	9 25
7½	Bangor-on-Dee .... ,,	9 21	12 8	2 38	3 48	6 11	7 31	9 31
10½	Marchwiel .... ,,	9 30	1215	2 45	3 55	6 20	7 40	9 40
12¾	**WREXHAM** (Central) arr.	9 35	1220	2 50	4 0	6 25	7 45	9 45

Moat Lane, Builth Wells, Brecon, etc.

Miles.	DOWN.	WEEK DAYS. am Mondays only. Workmen's Train.	H am	am	am	am	H am	pm	pm	pm	pm	pm	H pm	pm Mondays only.	pm	pm	pm	pm	pm	pm	SUN. am
—	**Moat Lane Junction**...dep	...	5 5	...	...	9 50	1120	..	1220	...	...	...	2 15		...	5 10	8 25	...	9 20	...	7 50
2	Llandinam ... ... ,,	...	*	...	...	9 55	...	...	1225	...	...	...	*		...	5 15	8 30	...	*	...	7 55
4¾	Dolwen ... ... ,,	...	*	...	...	10 2	...	...	1232	...	...	...	*		...	5 22	8 38	...	*	..	8 1
7½	**LLANIDLOES** ... arr	...	5 25	...	...	10 10	...	...	1240	...	...	...	2 32		...	5 27	8 45	...	9 40	...	8 7
	dep	5 15	5 27	...	8 15	10 15	1135	...		...	...	...	2 35		...	5 30		...		...	8 10
10¾	Tylwch ... ... ,,	...	5 35	...	8 23	10 25	...	...	...	...	...	...	2 44		...	5 37	...	...	...	...	8 18
14¾	Pantydwr ... ... ,,	...	5 45	...	8 31	10 35	...	...	...	...	...	...	2 54		...	5 45	...	...	...	...	8 27
16	St. Harmons ... ... ,,	...	*	...	*	10 40	...	...	...	...	...	...	*		...	*	...	..	...	...	*
21½	Rhayader ... ... ,,	5 45	6 2	...	8 50	11 0	1159	...	...	...	...	...	3 11		...	6 5	...	...	...	...	8 43
24¾	Doldowlod... ... ,,		6 9	...	8 59	11 10	...	...	...	...	...	...	3 18		...	6 13	...	...	...	...	8 51.
28¾	Newbridge-on-Wye ... ,,		6 18	...	9 10	11 25	...	...	...	...	...	...	3 26		...	6 22	...	...	...	...	9 0
32¾	**Builth Road** ... arr		6 27	...	9 20	11 35	1218	...	...	...	...	...	3 34		...	6 30	...	...	...	...	9 7
	dep		6 29	...	9 30	11 40	1228	...	...	...	1 5	...	3 45	4 15	6 5	6 38	...	...	...	...	9 8
34¼	**BUILTH WELLS** ... arr		6 33	...	9 34	11 45	1231	...	...	...	1 10	...	3 49	4 20	6 10	6 42	...	...	...	...	9 12
	dep		6 35	...	9 35		1237	...	...	...	1 12	...	3 53			6 45	...	...	...	...	9 16
38¾	Aberedw ... ... ,,		*	...	*	...	...	...	...	...	1 21	...	*	...	...	*	...	...	...	...	*
41	Erwood ... ... ,,		6 50	...	9 50	...	...	...	...	...	1 27	...	4 6	...	...	6 58	...	...	...	...	9 32
45¼	Boughrood ... ... ,,		7 2	...	10 0	...	...	...	...	...	1 40	...	4 16	...	...	7 8	...	...	...	...	9 43
48	**Three Cocks Junct** arr		7 7	...	10 5	...	...	...	...	...	1 46	...	4 22	...	...	7 14	...	...	...	...	9 51
	dep		7 9	...	10 6	...	...	...	...	...	1 52	...	4 27	...	...	7 15	...	...	...	...	9 53
50½	Talgarth ... ... ,,		7 14	...	10 11	...	...	...	...	...	1 58	...	4 33	...	...	7 20	...	...	...	...	9 58
53	Trefeinon ... ... ,,		*	...	*	...	...	...	...	...	*	...	...	...	...	*	...	...	...	..	*
56	**Talyllyn Junction** ... arr		7 27	...	10 23	...	1‖20	...	..	...	2 10	...	4 45	...	...	7 33	...	...	...	...	1011
	dep		7 35	...	10 50	...		...	...	...	2 15	...	4 50	...	...	7 35	...	...	...	...	1013
60	**BRECON** ... ...arr		7 45	...	11 0	...	...	...	...	...	2 25	...	5 0	...	...	7 45	...	...	...	...	1023

For Notes see Page 9.

MAIN LINE—Aberystwyth and Whitchurch.

Miles.	UP.		WEEK DAYS.																			SUN.	
								H	H					H		H	H			H			
			am	am	am	am	am	am	am	am	am	pm	pm	pm	pm	pm	pm	pm	pm	pm	pm	pm	pm
	ABERYSTWYTH	dep.	...	...	...	7 15	8 40	9 10	9 35	10 0	11 5	1215	...	1 0	...	2 15	2 45	2 55	5 40	6§25	8 25	6 25	...
4½	Bow Street	,,	...	...	...	7 25	8 50	...	O O	1010	11 16	...	...	...	...	...	...	3 5	5 50	...	8 35	6 35	...
6	Llanfihangel	,,	...	...	...	7 30	8 54	...	O O	1015	*	...	...	...	...	...	...	3 10	5 57	...	*	6 39	...
8½	Borth	,,	...	...	...	7 35	8 58	B	9 53	1020	11 25	1233	...	B	...	2 33	3 5	3 15	6 10	6g43	8 45	6 43	...
10½	Ynyslas	,,	...	...	...	7 40	9 5	...	...	1024	11 29	...	...	...	...	...	...	3 20	6 14	...	8 50	6 47	...
16	Glandyfi	,,	...	...	...	7 52	9 16	...	O O	1036	11 41	...	...	...	...	...	...	3 35	6 25	...	9 4	7 0	...
16¾	Dovey Jc.	arr.	...	...	...	7 55	9 19	9 45	10 9	1038	...	1249	Tuesdays only. Third Class only.	1 35	...	2 50	3 23	3 38	6 27	7§ 0	9 7	...	...
		dep.	...	...	...	8 0	9 22	9 53	1014	1050	...	1255		1 50	...	2 55	3 27		6 31	7§ 6	9 8	...	...
20½	Machynlleth	arr.	...	...	...	8 8	9 30	10 0	1021	11 0	11 49	1 2		1 58	...	3 10	3 34	...	6 38	7§13	9 15	7 10	...
		dep.	...	...	...	8 15		10 4	1026		11 54	1 5		2 3	...	3 12	3 36	...	6 40	7§17		7 17	...
25¾	Cemmes Road	,,	...	...	...	8 25	...	1013	B	...	12 4	1 15		...	...	...	...	...	6 50	7§26	...	7 26	...
31	Llanbrynmair	,,	...	...	...	8 37	...	...	B	...	12 16	...		...	...	...	...	...	7 2	7§38	...	7 38	...
34½	Talerddig	,,	...	...	...	*	...	...	...	...	12 29	...		...	...	...	...	...	*	K	...	*	...
36½	Carno	,,	...	...	...	8 51	...	...	B	...	12 33	...		...	...	...	...	...	7 17	7§52	...	7 52	...
40¾	Pontdolgoch	,,	...	...	...	8 58	...	...	...	...	*	...		...	...	...	...	...	7 25	...	...	8 0	...
42¼	Caersws	,,	...	...	...	9 5	...	...	...	...	12 45	...		...	...	...	...	...	7 30	8§ 4	...	8 4	...
43¼	Moat Lane Jc.	arr.	...	...	...	9 9	...	...	1110	...	12 47	1 47	☞	2 51	...	3 58	...	...	7 33	8§ 6	...	8 6	...
		dep.	...	...	6 55	9 15	...	...		...	12 52	1 50	...	2 55	...	4 2	...	...	7 38	8§11	..	8 11	...
48½	NEWTOWN	,,	...	...	7 8	9 30	...	11 0	...	...	1 5	2 4	2 20	3 5	...	4 15	4 32	...	7 54	8§26	...	8 26	...
55½	... Kerry	dep.	...	Wednesdays only.	6‡50	8 40	...	...	...	...	12e45	...	2 5	...	...	3S50	...	...	7 0	...	...	...	...
		arr.	...		7‡50	10 5	...	...	...	...	1e45	...	3 5	...	...	5S10	...	...	9 20	9 20	...	...	...
51¾	Abermule	dep.	...		7 17	9 39	...	...	...	...	1 15	...	2 33	...	...	S	...	...	8 3	8§35	...	8 35	...
55½	Montgomery	,,	...		7 25	9 47	...	O	...	...	1 27	...	2 42	B	...	4 32	...	...	8 10	8§44	...	8 44	...
57½	Forden	,,	...		7 30	9 51	...	...	...	...	1 31	...	2 46	...	...	...	...	...	8 15	...	...	8 48	...
61¾	WELSHPOOL	arr.	...		7 40	10 0	...	1125	...	...	1 40	2 27	2 56	3 30	...	4 45	4 56	p m	8 25	8 55	...	8 55	...
		dep.	...		7 45	1020	...	1140	...	...		2 32		LONDON EXPRESS.	3 35	4 55		5 55	8 30	9 0	...	9 0	...
64½	Buttington	,,	...		7 50	1025	...	...	...	...	...	NORTH EXPRESS.	...		3 40	...	...	6 2	8 35	K	...	9 5	...
66½	Pool Quay	,,	...		7 55	1030	...	...	...	...	...		...		3 44	...	...	6 7	8 40	K	...	*	...
68¼	Arddleen	,,	...		Wed	F	...	...	...	...	...		...		Mon	...	...	Mon	...	...	...	...	...
70	Four Crosses	,,	...		8 5	1040	...	...	...	...	...		...		3 52	...	...	6 17	8 48	K	...	*	...
71½	Llanymynech	arr.	...	☞	8 8	1045	...	...	...	p m	...		...		3 56	...	...	6 22	8 52	9 20	...	9 20	...
80½	Llanfyllin	dep.	...	7 30	7 30	1015	...	...	...	1 45	...		...		...	...	...	5 55	7 20	...	...	...	...
		arr.	...	...	8 55	1135	...	...	...	...	...		...		4 35	...	...	7 0	...	...	...	...	...
71½	Llanymynech	dep.	...	8 5	8 10	1050	...	..	...	2 15	...		...		3 58	...	...	6 25	8 55	9 22	...	9 21	...
72½	Pant	,,	...	...	*	1054	...	...	...	*	...		...		*	...	...	*	8 58	...	...	...	...
73½	Lynclys	,,	...	...	8 19	11 0	...	...	...	2 25	...		...		4 7	...	...	6 38	9 2	K	...	9 26	...
77½	OSWESTRY	arr.	...	8 20	8 27	1110	...	1210	p m	2 35	...	2 57	...		4 15	5 20	...	6 50	9 10	9 35	...	9 35	...
		dep	6 5		8 35	1125	...	1215	1 50		...	3 2	...		4 20	5 25	...			9 40	...	9 40	...
79¼	Whittington	,,	6 10	...	8 39	1129	...	...	1 55	...	...	...	...	...	4 25	...	...	...	...	*	...	*	...
82¾	Frankton	,,	6 18	...	8 47	1137	...	...	2 3	...	..	...	...	...	4 33	...	...	...	...	*	...	*	...
84¾	Ellesmere	,,	6 25	...	8 55	1145	...	1235	2 10	...	...	3 20	...	...	4 42	5 46	...	...	...	10 0	...	10 0	...
87¾	Welshampton	,,	*	...	9 2	1152	...	...	*	...	...	...	...	...	4 49	...	...	...	...	*	...	*	...
89	Bettisfield	,,	6 35	...	9 6	1155	...	...	2 19	...	...	...	...	...	4 53	...	...	...	...	*	...	*	...
92¾	Fenns's Bank	,,	6 47	...	9 16	12 5	...	...	2 28	...	...	...	...	...	5 3	...	...	...	...	*	...	*	...
95¾	WHITCHURCH	arr.	6 55	...	9 25	1212	...	1255	2 35	...	...	3 40	...	...	5 10	6 10	...	...	...	10 25	...	1025	...

Llanfyllin Branch.

No Sunday Trains.

Miles.	DOWN.		WEEK DAYS.						
			am	am	pm	pm	pm		
—	Llanymynech	dep.	8 25	1110	4 10	6 35	8 0	...	...
3¾	Llansaintffraid	,,	8 35	1118	4 18	6 43	8 10	...	...
5	Llanfechain	,,	8 42	1125	4 25	6 50	8 18	...	...
7	Bryngwyn	,,	*	*	*	*	*	...	...
8¾	Llanfyllin	arr.	8 55	1135	4 35	7 0	8 30	...	...

Miles	UP.		WEEK DAYS.								
				am		am	pm	pm	pm		
...	Llanfyllin	dep.	...	7 30	...	10 15	1 45	5 55	7 20	...	...
2	Bryngwyn	,,	...	*	...	*	*	*	*	...	...
3¾	Llanfechain	,,	...	7 40	...	10 25	1 55	6 5	7 32	...	...
5½	Llansaintffraid	,,	...	7 47	...	10 32	2 2	6 12	7 40	...	...
8¾	Llanymynech	arr.	...	7 55	..	10 40	2 10	6 20	7 50	...	...

Moat Lane, Builth Wells, Brecon, etc.

Miles.	UP.		WEEK DAYS.																			SUN.	
												H		H							H		
			am	am	am	am	am	am	am	am	am	am	pm	pm	pm	pm	pm	pm	pm	pm	pm	pm	
	BRECON	dep.	...	6 40	...	...	...	...	...	1040	...	...	...	...	1 20	...	...	...	4 25	...	5 35	5 30	...
4	Talyllyn Jc.	arr.	...	6 50	...	...	...	...	...	1050	...	...	...	...	1 30	...	...	...	4 35	...	5 45	5 40	...
		dep.	...	6 51	...	...	...	...	...	11 0	...	11‖40	...	1‖20	1 33	...	...	...	4 45	...	5 46	5 41	...
7	Trefeinon	,,	...	*	...	...	...	...	...	*	...	...	...	...	*	...	...	...	*	...	*	*	...
9¼	Talgarth	,,	...	7 4	...	...	...	...	...	1113	...	...	Saturdays only. Workmen's Train.	...	1 46	...	...	...	5 0	...	5 57	5 54	...
11¾	Three Cocks Junction	arr.	...	7 9	...	...	...	...	...	1118	...	...		...	1 51	...	...	...	5 5	...	6 2	5 59	...
		dep.	...	7 12	...	...	...	...	...	1120	...	...		...	1 55	...	...	...	5 10	...	6 3	6 0	...
14½	Boughrood	,,	...	7 19	...	...	...	...	...	1128	...	...		...	2 1	...	...	...	5 16	...	6 9	6 6	...
18¾	Erwood	,,	...	7 27	...	...	...	...	...	1135	...	...		...	2 9	...	...	...	5 25	...	6 17	6 15	...
21½	Aberedw	,,	...	*	...	...	...	...	...	*	...	...		...	*	...	...	...	*	...	...	*	...
25½	BUILTH WELLS	arr.	...	7 42	...	...	...	...	...	1150	...	12 18		2 0	2 22	...	...	...	5 40	...	6 30	6 30	...
		dep	...	7 45	...	8 45	...	...	...	1155	...	12 23		2 10	2 25	...	3 40	...	5 45	...	6 34	6 32	...
27	Builth Road	arr.	...	7 50	...	8 50	...	...	...	12 0	...	12 27		2 14	2 30	...	3 45	...	5 50	...	6 38	...	...
		dep	...	7 52	...		...	...	...	1220	...	12 35	☞	2 20	2 35	...		...		...	6 40	6 36	...
31	Newbridge-on-Wye	,,	...	8 0	...	...	...	...	...	1228	...	...		...	2 43	...	☞ Mondays only	...	...	...	6 47	6 43	...
35	Doldowlod	,,	...	8 8	...	...	...	...	...	1236	...	...		...	2 51	...		...	...	...	*	*	...
38¼	Rhayader	,,	...	8 18	...	...	...	...	...	1247	...	...	2 15	...	3 8	...		...	...	...	7 6	7 2	...
43¾	St. Harmons	,,	...	*	...	...	...	...	...	...	...	...	...	...	*	...		...	...	...	*	*	...
45	Pantydwr	,,	...	8 31	...	...	...	...	...	1 0	...	...	...	...	3 22	...		...	...	...	*	7 15	...
49	Tylwch	,,	...	8 41	...	...	...	...	...	1 10	...	...	...	...	3 31	...		...	...	...	7 29	7 25	...
52¼	LLANIDLOES	arr.	...	8 47	...	...	...	...	...	1 16	...	1 30	2 50	3 8	3 37	...		...	...	...	7 35	7 31	...
		dep.	6 35	8 50	...	...	...	1145	...	1 19	...	1 35		3 13	3 40	...		...	...	...	7 40	7 35	...
55	Dolwen	,,	6 40	8 56	...	...	...	1150	...	*	...	...	...	..	3 45	...		...	...	...	7 46	7 41	...
57¾	Llandinam	,,	6 47	9 3	...	...	...	1159	...	*	...	...	...	...	3 52	...		...	...	...	7 55	7 50	...
59¾	Moat Lane Jc.	arr.	6 53	9 7	...	...	...	12 5	...	1 35	...	1 50	...	3 28	3 56	...		...	...	...	8 0	7 55	...

FOR NOTES SEE PAGE 9.

Above:
Aberystwyth, though comparatively small, was the largest Cambrian station. Like those serving many small towns and resorts, it was well situated close to the centre and at Aberystwyth holidaymakers had only a short walk to the promenade. Cambrian No 34, one of the company's most unsuccessful locomotives, awaits departure with an up train. It was one of six 4-4-0 tanks bought from the Metropolitan Railway when it was electrified in 1905. No 34 was rebuilt as a tender locomotive in 1914. A striking cluster of six signals on a stout post dominates the down platform. Left is a train of coaches tailed by a GWR open wagon standing in the Manchester & Milford platform. *Tony Icke Collection*

Left:
Oswestry remained a busy station until its Beeching demise. An SLS special, marking the end of passenger services over the Oswestry, Ellesmere and Whitchurch section of the main line and the Llanfyllin branch in January 1965, is headed by ex-GWR 4-6-0 No 7802 *Bradley Manor*. The ex-GWR Gobowen branch bay platform (centre) and goods shed (right) can be seen. *R. W. Miller*

Welsh Railway — English Headquarters

This portrait is affectionate because the Cambrian Railways — plural through being formed by amalgamation of small companies — is still regarded in that vein by countless people today, some 80 years after its demise.

It is also the way that I remember it from boyhood, despite getting a finger trapped in a carriage door at Dovey Junction during a day trip with my parents from Aberystwyth to Barmouth in summer 1938.

Almost half a century later, my enthusiasm led me to blow myself into retirement from the BBC with a 'Thunderer Patent' brass whistle inscribed 'Cam Rly Co'. It lies before me as I begin this portrait, in which I shall concentrate on the pre-Grouping years down to 1922, because so much has been written about its fate in Great Western, British Rail and other eras and down to the present day.

The Cambrian, which never had a nickname, was the largest, though far from the busiest, of the Welsh independent railway companies, all full of character and most of great charm, which opened up much of the Principality in Victorian days. It ended the isolation of many small villages and scattered communities, with branches and miles of main lines stretching from the English border at Whitchurch to the coast of Cardigan Bay between Aberystwyth

Below:
Through the years, several pictures which are now classics have captured the spirit of the line. No 6, an 0-6-0 built by Sharp, Stewart of Manchester in 1883, heads an up train at Llanymynech in 1904, nine years after rebuilding. *LGRP*

and Pwllheli, and through mid-Wales and the Wye Valley to Brecon.

It served only one large industrial town, Wrexham, and that was relatively small and the Cambrian's lifeline to it was tenuous and single.

Whitchurch, a market town in the quiet countryside of north Shropshire, is only 13 miles south of Crewe, hub of the London & North Western Railway, biggest of the English companies with which the Cambrian was increasingly favourably compared, despite a huge difference in size. The Cambrian publicly named the LNWR as its 'closest ally', with junctions at Whitchurch, with the Shrewsbury & Welshpool Joint at Buttington, near Welshpool, Builth Road and Afon Wen.

The Cambrian described its association with the GWR as being 'also very intimate'. It exchanged a considerable amount of traffic at Oswestry, Buttington, Aberystwyth (with the Manchester & Milford) and Dolgelley. The Cambrian met the Great Central at Wrexham and the Midland at Three Cocks Junction and had running powers to Hereford. They were never used.

Other Cambrian running powers included ones over the Brecon & Merthyr from Talyllyn Junction to Brecon, and over the LNWR into Whitchurch station. Running powers between Builth Road and Llandrindod Wells were never exercised.

The Cambrian, which had close relations with the B&M, Rhymney, Taff Vale and Barry Railways, was always conscious of being a Welsh railway with its headquarters in England at Oswestry just across the border in Shropshire. In a 1914 guide published by

Above:
The mountains to the south have always formed an impressive backcloth of the 800yd Barmouth Viaduct of 1866. A train headed by 2-4-0 No 54 is completing the crossing of the opening span in about 1899 — the year the span was rebuilt. *LGRP*

Above right:
Cambrian Railway's No 7 *Llanerchydol* — named after a director's home — belonged to the 'Volunteer' class of seven Sharp, Stewart 0-4-2 tender engines. Aberdovey, a station dominated by a high wooden footbridge, was not reached by the Coast line until 1861 — the year after the locomotive was built.
LPC

Right:
The 2.43pm up stopping train is dwarfed by the historic castle as it departs from Harlech on 15 July 1911. It is headed by 'Beaconsfield' class 4-4-0 No 50, dating from 1891. *H. W. Burmam/R. W. Miller collection*

the Canadian Pacific Railway to encourage emigrants to visit 'the old country', the Cambrian asserted its Welsh character: 'A few minutes after leaving Oswestry the train crosses the border of England and Wales and whatever point on the Cambrian Railways may afterwards be visited, the tourist would remain in Wales.'

It is unlikely that expats who may have read the Guide saw Wales through its carriage windows, for only weeks after publication, World War 1 broke out.

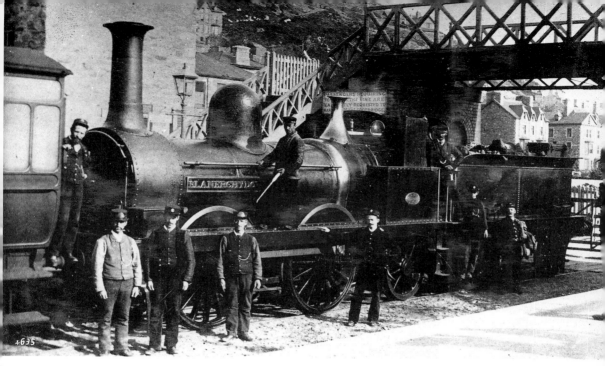

Left:
Oswestry, where, deep into the Great Western years, enthusiasts travelled miles to see former Cambrian locomotives still working local goods and branch passenger trains. GWR 2-4-0T No 1197 — ex-CR No 59 (Sharp, Stewart 1866) — with a Tanat Valley service in summer 1938. The tank survived another decade. *R. J. Buckley/ R. W. Miller collection*

Centre left:
Llynclys Junction with the Porthywaen branch, from which the Tanat Valley branch stemmed from 1904, lay 3½ miles south of Oswestry. The water tank and coaling stages on the opposite side of the sharply curved junction were used by small locomotives shunting quarry and other sidings. A wintry Edwardian scene of 1904, after a light snowfall on the hills to the west. *LGRP*

Below left:
All local trains stopped at Llynclys but Pant, which also served the thinly populated country between Oswestry and Welshpool, was only a conditional stop for several services. *LGRP*

Right:
Llanymynech was an historic junction where the PSNWR, later the Shropshire & Montgomeryshire, arrived from Shrewsbury (Abbey) and continued towards Blodwell Junction over a sharp curve west. From 1896 a new curve gave direct access from the 'Potts' route to the Llanfyllin branch. Soon after Grouping, the GWR abandoned the section between the new curve and Blodwell Junction, leaving sole access to the Tanat Valley from Llynclys. *LGRP*

Advancing into Mid-Wales

When I started researching the two-volume history of the Cambrian Railways in the early 1960s, I found myself in a most appropriate setting: the British Transport Historical Records office in Porchester Road, at the approach to Paddington station. The building was uninspiring but the setting was full of nostalgia. From a fire escape I watched steam locomotives being turned in Ranelagh Bridge yard far below and the 'Cambrian Coast Express' was among titled trains that ran by.

The mountains and Cardigan Bay seemed remote but I quickly got to know the history of their railways as I became absorbed in Cambrian board minutes, reports to directors and traffic statistics.

First, I had to untangle the mystery of why early railways were not built in mid-Wales until a decade and more after the Railway Mania of the 1840s, which led to many equally sparsely populated areas of Britain being put quickly on the railway map.

The Cambrian Railways would never have existed in the shape into which the company finally grew if the early Welsh promoters had achieved their aspirations. For their foremost aim was to cross Wales to provide a route between England and Ireland, rather than simply serve glorious, but empty, countryside.

The concept was first considered by the Irish Railway Commission set up by the Government in 1836. A year later C. B. Vignoles, the prominent engineer, was asked to survey a route from Shrewsbury to the hamlet of Porth Dinlleyn, where a sheltered harbour, so essential in the days of sail, was to be built. He suggested a railway through the small towns of the Dee Valley — Llangollen, Bala and Dolgelley — to the coast at Barmouth and then heading north through Portmadoc and across the Lleyn Peninsula.

It was a scheme of sufficient importance to be shown among projected 'rail roads' on contemporary maps. They also showed the line of the Montgomeryshire Canal, authorised in 1794, which was one of the main routes by which goods were taken into the Severn Valley and the products of its small but growing industries were exported. The canals of mid-Wales and a number of associated tramroads are well documented and worthy of study.

A terminus at Porth Dinlleyn was attractive to early promoters because it avoided bridging the fast-flowing, tidal Menai Strait. It was favoured by

Brunel, who was also working on a London-Ireland link. But while Vignoles planned to keep to the valleys, Brunel took to the hills with a route from Worcester, breasting Talerddig and then burrowing under the formidable 3,000ft-high mountain barrier of Cader Idris to reach the coast. His bold yet hardly practical scheme was forgotten when the Chester & Crewe promoters asked George Stephenson to survey an 84-mile line along the coastal strip between Chester and Holyhead. It was to be level for almost 70 miles. Bridging the Menai Strait was regarded as practical, if costly.

The Chester & Holyhead was authorised in 1844 and opened in 1850. Meanwhile, mid-Wales was left without any prospect of relief from isolation until 1853, when a scheme for linking the market towns of Llanidloes and Newtown was mooted. Compared with the Chester & Holyhead and the projects of Vignoles and Brunel, it could hardly have been more modest. But it was a springboard for schemes which within a decade created a system, mostly single, of some 295 miles, and formed the core of what became the Cambrian Railways.

Another grandiose scheme of the 1845 Mania was the Manchester & Milford Railway, designed by the engineer John Rastrick to import American cotton via Milford Haven and reach Lancashire via Llanidloes, Newtown and Crewe. Eventually only 41

Above:
For years Welshpool was a market town with contrasting railway stations. Viewed from the yard, the exterior of the Oswestry & Newtown station gave it a vague air of a country mansion, while the terminus of the narrow gauge Welshpool & Llanfair Railway was hardly more than that of a cottage. *P. J. Sharpe*

Above right:
Exceptionally painstaking research would be needed to find out when public timetables first revealed that Montgomery station was nearly two miles from the village. The distance may have been responsible for the presence, in late Victorian days, of an open-seat, two-horse bus after the arrival of an LNWR train headed by an 'Albion' class 2-4-0. Tall up and down signals are placed on a single post. *R. W. Miller collection*

Below right:
People living in small towns and isolated villages were well served by the Cambrian, with most branches having several weekday services each way. The Kerry branch platform at Abermule handled at least four on most weekdays, the last evening train up the steeply graded branch not leaving Abermule until 8.55pm. *LGRP*

miles from Pencader to Aberystwyth were opened in 1867. The company, with its eight locomotives and 14 carriages, was taken over by the GWR in 1906.

THE OPENING CEREMONY AT MACHYNLLETH.

Llanidloes & Newtown Railway

Curtain raiser to the formation of the Llanidloes & Newtown Railway, the first of the group of small and independent companies which became the Cambrian, was an ambitious plan to build a railway from Shrewsbury to Aberystwyth called the Montgomeryshire Railway. It was thrown out by the House of Commons, whose members preferred the more local Llanidloes & Newtown.

But that was dismissed in the Lords because of a survey by Rice Hopkins, whose father had laid the Penydarren Tramway in South Wales, the first line in the world to use a locomotive. The survey included levels which at one point showed the railway running 18 feet below the level of the Severn. The river was the main obstacle to the line, which had to cross it four times on wooden trestle bridges.

A revised Bill was accepted in August 1853 but it was not until 1 September 1859 that 600 men who had worked on the 12 miles of single track attended 'a grand festal entertainment' to mark the railway's opening the day before. It was held in Llandinam. The hosts, described by a local paper as 'the liberal and spirited contractors', were two notable personalities of early Welsh railways: David Davies, who was born in Llandinam and later became an international figure of the South Wales coal industry, and Thomas Savin, a speculator, who came from Oswestry.

Locomotives had to be delivered by low wagons pulled over rough roads by teams of horses. Coaches arrived on the Montgomeryshire Canal, a branch of the Shropshire Union. All work stopped on Sundays — and at many other times it seems, for construction was halted for months at a time because of money shortages.

Above:
Ceremonies associated with the construction and opening of lines sometimes reflected social conditions. An advertisement for the first sod cutting of the Oswestry, Ellesmere & Whitchurch Railway in 1862 (more than a year after authorisation) noted that the 'poorer women' of Oswestry and neighbourhood would be provided with tea in the bowling green tent the next day.

Right:
The 23-mile Newtown & Machynlleth Railway, opened in January 1863, did not actually link the towns, because the eastern four miles between Newtown and a junction created at Moat Lane had been built by the Llanidloes & Newtown Railway. *Author's collection*

Oswestry & Newtown Railway

After its opening in 1859 the L&N remained isolated until the opening of the Oswestry & Newtown Railway in 1860-1. Again, Davies and Savin were prominent in its promotion, as they were either separately or in partnership for construction of all the lines which formed the Cambrian. Had it not been for their willingness to accept a substantial part of payments in shares, and sometimes to find a required Parliamentary deposit themselves, it is doubtful if much of the Cambrian would ever have been built. Shares were also accepted in part-payment for locomotives (Sharp, Stewart & Co) and rails (Ebbw Vale Co).

The O&N was authorised in 1855 but construction did not begin until summer 1857, when Victorian pomp and ceremony included the firing from Powis Castle, Welshpool, of guns captured by

Clive of India. In his original Oakwood Press history of the Cambrian, published in 1954, R. W. Kidner observed, 'it is tempting to laugh at Welsh railway ceremonies, but rather should one stand back in awe.'

The O&N was a line of far greater substance and importance than the L&N, for besides being the spearhead of a route from England into mid-Wales, it was joined in 1862 by the 16-mile Shrewsbury & Welshpool Railway. This company, acquired by the GWR and LNWR jointly in 1865, forged the shortest route between London, the Midlands and mid-Wales.

The S&W gained access to Welshpool, where it joined the O&N, using 2½ miles of running powers from Buttington, under the slopes of Breidden Hill. Originally called Cefn, it was a station of rural extravagance, with the O&N and S&W each having double platforms.

The O&N stemmed from the GWR at Oswestry and the promoters' aims of linking growing towns in the Severn Valley was reflected in the title in the Act of Incorporation: Oswestry, Welchpool (a common contemporary spelling) & Newtown Railway. A number of stations were built to serve small villages and in later years the Cambrian opened others, even though there were few people living near enough to use them. It was a policy that showed a small company like the Cambrian cared about small, isolated communities — an attitude in sharp contrast to that of the LNWR, which in its guidebooks sneered at 'some unimportant stations' between Oswestry and Welshpool.

For years Cambrian passengers were mystified by a large platform noticeboard at Welshpool exhorting them to 'Change for Shrewsbury, Stafford, Birmingham and London'. But its message was sound, for Euston provided the main route between London and the coast until the GWR opened its direct Paddington-Birmingham (Snow Hill) route via Aynho in 1910. The LNWR showed Euston-Aberystwyth services in public timetables headed 'Stafford, Shrewsbury & Welshpool'.

Newtown & Machynlleth Railway

In the late 1850s, 23 miles of railway were needed to link Newtown and Machynlleth, the L&N having already taken a railway five miles west through the Valley from Newtown. There was no Parliamentary opposition to the Newtown & Machynlleth Railway — the third to carry Newtown in its title — incorporated in 1857 from the L&N at Moat Lane to Machynlleth.

The contractors were Davies & Savin but the line was built by Davies alone after he split from Savin. The concept of a 120ft-deep cutting at the watershed at Talerddig was that of the engineer, Benjamin Piercy. A cutting was preferred to a tunnel because of yielding rock for bridges and embankments. Piercy was praised for his boldness, the *Gossiping Guide to Wales* noting in 1879 that

CEREMONY OF
Cutting the First Sod
Of the OSWESTRY SECTION of the
OSWESTRY, ELLESMERE, & WHITCHURCH
RAILWAY,
On Thursday, the 4th September, 1862,
AT OSWESTRY.

COMMITTEE OF MANAGEMENT:
CHAIRMAN—David Lloyd, Esq., Mayor of Oswestry.

Mr. Alderman Rogers	Mr. Councillor Dale	Mr. John Morris, builder
„ Alderman Morris	„ Councillor Saunders	„ David Rees, banker
„ Alderman Minshall	„ Councillor E. W. Thomas	„ Dr. Fuller
„ Councillor Phillips	„ Councillor John Thomas	„ Mr. I. F. Whitridge
„ Councillor Hilditch	„ Benjamin Roberts	„ Henry G. Weaver

TREASURER—Mr. Henry Davies. | HON. SEC.—Mr. Askew Roberts.

PROGRAMME:
THE DEMONSTRATION WILL BE COMMENCED AT 11 O'CLOCK IN THE MORNING, BY
A PROCESSION,
WHICH WILL
FORM ON THE BAILEY HEAD,
IN THE FOLLOWING ORDER:—

Brass Band.
King Oswald and Philanthropic Lodges of Odd-fellows.
Flags and Banners.
Band.
The Mayor and Corporation of Oswestry.
The Friends and Well-wishers.
The Railway Rifle Corps, headed by their Band.
The Directors, Officials, and Invited Guests.
Band.
The Court Duke of Cornwall Order of Foresters.
Flags and Banners.
The Ancient Briton Sun Friendly Society.
Drum and Fife Band.
The Juvenile Branch of Odd-fellows.
Flags and Banners.
The Children of the various Schools.
The Workmen.

The Friendly Societies will meet in the Horse Market, at Eleven o'clock, the Juvenile Lodge and the School Children on the Bailey Head, and the Friends and Well-wishers in the Powis Hall, so as to be marshalled in proper order to accompany the Mayor and Corporation from the Council Chamber, as the clock strikes Twelve.

The Procession will march down Bailey Street, through the Cross, up Church Street, down Lower Brook Street, where it will turn off opposite the Dispensary, along Roft Street to the New Church, and up Salop Road to the Cross Keys, and thence through the New Road to the SHELF BANK FIELD, where

THE FIRST SOD WILL BE CUT
By Miss KINCHANT, of Park Hall.

The Barrow and Spade will be presented by Mr. SAVIN, the Contractor, and after the ceremony, a few complimentary speeches will be delivered from the Platform erected for the occasion.

At the conclusion of the Ceremony, the Procession will again form, with the Foresters and Sun Friendly Societies in front, the Odd-fellows bringing up the rear. In returning, the Procession will march up Beatrice Street and Albion Hill, to the Bailey Head, where it will separate. The Children will then be supplied with buns, &c., in the Powis Hall. At THREE o'clock,

A COLD COLLATION
WILL TAKE PLACE ON THE
WYNNSTAY ARMS BOWLING GREEN, IN A SPLENDID MARQUEE,
Erected for the occasion, and to which the Ladies are specially invited to attend, as well as Gentlemen.

After the Luncheon a select number of toasts will be proposed and responded to, after which the Tent will be cleared for a

RURAL FETE,
To which the Luncheon Tickets will admit. The Admission to those who have not attended the Luncheon will be One Shilling, by tickets, which may be purchased at the Bar of the Hotel.

Tickets for the Collation, 5s. each, may be had from Mr. Baugh, Ellesmere; at the Bar of the Wynnstay Arms Hotel, or from the *Advertiser* Office, Bailey Head, Oswestry.

The Committee hope that the persons composing the Procession will assist in keeping to the order of the Programme, both in going to, and returning from, the field, so as to prevent confusion.

☞ It is particularly requested that Ladies and Gentlemen intending to purchase tickets for the Collation, will do so on or before Monday, the 1st of September, that the Committee may have some idea how many guests they will have to provide for.

SPECIAL NOTICE.—The poorer women of the town and neighbourhood will be provided with Tea in the Tent on the Bowling Green, on Friday, the 5th September. Tickets may be had from any member of the Committee.

ASKEW ROBERTS, PRINTER, BAILEY HEAD, OSWESTRY.

the idea would have 'broken the hearts of many contractors'.

Piercy's alignment climbed from just over 400ft above sea level in the Severn Valley to Talerddig summit at 693ft with a maximum gradient of 1 in 71. The descent to almost sea level at Machynlleth was slightly more dramatic, the first four miles being at 1 in 52/60. The N&M was completed in January 1863 within set time limits.

Left:
The most striking section of the N&M was Talerddig rock cutting, reputed to have been the deepest in the world when it was constructed. Heavy trains were always banked to the summit, 693ft above sea level. In August 1913 the 9.5am Aberystwyth-Whitchurch is headed by 4-4-0 No 95 and banked by 4-4-0 No 72. Between them is sandwiched a motley collection of coaches.
LCGB

Below left:
A commercial postcard showed Aston 4-4-0 No 64 climbing Talerddig. The card was No 4 in a 'Trains in Motion' series published by J. M. Tomlinson of Poulton-le-Fylde. It was intended for enthusiasts, being captioned: 'The warning distant (G W Rly)'.
R. W. Miller collection

Formation of the Cambrian Railways

The aspirations of the mid-Wales promoters during the years the N&M was under construction became clear from *Murray's Hand-Book, North Wales*, 1861 edition: 'The Oswestry, Welshpool, Newtown & Llanidloes bids fair to become a great trunk line when the other sections are completed, which will unite it to the Mid-Wales or Central Wales railways. When this takes place a continuous and uninterrupted route will be furnished from Manchester to Milford Haven, proceeding via Oswestry, Newtown and Llanidloes to Rhayader, Builth, Llandovery, Llandeilo and Carmarthen.'

It was not to be for a number of reasons, not least because of events in June and July 1864, which were the most productive months in the history of mid-Wales railways. On 23 June, the Aberystwyth & Welsh Coast Railway (page 23) was completed between Machynlleth and Aberystwyth. On 25 July, the Cambrian Railways Company was formed by the amalgamation of the Llanidloes & Newtown, Oswestry & Newtown, Newtown & Machynlleth and Oswestry, Ellesmere & Whitchurch companies. Two days later the OE&W was opened to complete the Cambrian main line of 95¾ miles from Whitchurch to Aberystwyth.

Oswestry, Ellesmere & Whitchurch Railway

The OE&W was incorporated after defeating the strongest opposition met by any of the constituent companies and having had, in its own words, 'to fight for every inch of ground'. The reason was that

it strategically challenged the Great Western Railway and, to a limited extent, invaded its territory.

The OE&W was promoted to give the expanding railways of mid-Wales a third outlet to England, via the Shrewsbury & Crewe line, which the LNWR had opened in September 1858 and was to double four years later. The OE&W bridged the Shrewsbury & Chester main line at Whittington, near Oswestry, which the S&C had reached with a branch from Gobowen, two miles north, in December 1848. Having put Oswestry on the railway map, the GWR opposed the OE&W because of the threat of mid-Wales traffic being routed via Whitchurch rather than Gobowen.

Parliament rejected the GWR case amid much local rejoicing, with Oswestry church bells being rung for two days, although there was less enthusiasm seven miles away at Ellesmere, the only intermediate town on the new line. Here nobody could be found to peal celebratory bells. But there were plenty of navvies on hand to start construction and within six months 11 miles of single track had been laid between Whitchurch and Ellesmere.

The stretch included the conquest of Whixall Moss, a bog almost three miles broad and often compared with Chat Moss on the Liverpool & Manchester Railway. Three hundred men laid the track on a raft of brushwood supported by timbers, prompting the *Gossiping Guide to Wales* to note that it created 'a solid road on which engines now run where man never walked before'. A Cambrian coat of arms incorporated into the brickwork of the modest station house at Frankton indicated that it was occupied not by the stationmaster, but a senior

company official who worked at Oswestry headquarters six miles away.

A major source of traffic during World War 1 and long afterwards was Park Hall, between Oswestry and Frankton. It grew to be one of the biggest Army camps in Britain, where troops trained in their thousands, and German prisoners of war were held in their own camp. The CR maintained and worked a short War Department branch serving the camp from 1 April 1918, under an agreement not signed until 11 January 1919 — two months after the Armistice. The Cambrian was empowered to take over from the War Department, stores and permanent way materials necessary for the work.

Fenn's Bank and Bettisfield, the first stations on leaving Whitchurch, were for years popular with Crewe railway workers escaping from the town for a day's fishing in the Shropshire Union Canal. They bought tickets from the LNWR quarter-fare privilege office in a wooden hut beside Crewe station.

Right:
Three coaches and 2-4-0 No 41 form the 6.10pm Machynlleth-Pwllheli, virtually an all stations stopper. It was allowed 3hr for the 57¼ miles. *LCGB*

Below:
With platforms as exposed to sea breezes as its neighbour Dovey Junction, Glandyfi was one of five small intermediate stations between the Junction and Aberystwyth. Despite its isolation, Glandyfi was busy enough for its wooden down platform to be extended with a solid surface and stronger railings. *LGRP*

Above:
Barmouth Junction. The Coast line from Dovey Junction comes in left and curves sharply to the embankment and Barmouth Viaduct (upper left). Dolgelley branch platforms with a down goods and beyond, an up train for Ruabon with the locomotive working tender first. The formation includes clerestory coaches, one with a roof-board, suggesting a through service to Birkenhead. *IAL/Bucknall Collection*

Coastal Conquest: Aberystwyth & Welsh Coast Railway

U nforgettable: Cardigan Bay viewed from the footplate of a 'Manor' class 4-6-0 hauling the midday express from Aberystwyth to Oswestry, as it descends the bank towards Borth on a cold, sunny, blustery, winter's day. Out to sea,

white-topped waves rolling towards the deserted shore. They reminded me that rough seas often endangered and hampered the builders of exposed stretches of line further north.

The Aberystwyth & Welsh Coast Railway had a complicated birth, being authorised in no fewer than 11 sections between 1861-5 and opened, also in a number of short sections, between 1863-9.

A 'monster train', run in summer 1864 to celebrate the 'connection of Aberystwyth with the rest of the world by railway', left Cambrian metals at Machynlleth because the A&WC was not absorbed until a year later due to legal delays. But relations remained friendly and the Cambrian worked it from opening.

The inaugural train stopped at Borth for 150 men associated with Wales and Welsh railways to enjoy a celebration lunch at the Cambrian Hotel. They saw a row of three-storey terraced houses dwarfing the

Below left:
Dovey Junction with a train from Machynlleth. Locomotive No 36 is one of the former Metropolitan 4-4-0 tanks. *IAL/Bucknall Collection*

Below:
On leaving Dovey Junction, the Coast line twists its way on a narrow ledge beside the shore of the estuary. No 86 heads a train of mixed stock forming a Welshpool-Pwllheli service about 1920. The stretch is near Penhelig. *H. W. Burman/R. W. Miller collection*

single-storey station building. It had been built by Savin and his brother in an attempt to develop the fishing village into a resort which would attract residents as well as holidaymakers.

A larger hotel was built at Aberystwyth, where the terminal, on a site of three acres, became the largest station on the Cambrian, with four platforms and four roads. The Manchester & Milford Railway had its own terminus by the harbour. It had running powers into the larger station but because of access disputes it used no more than a short bay platform. In 1922 Aberystwyth was enlarged to five platforms and seven roads.

The Coast Section:
Dovey Junction-Pwllheli

The 57-mile Coast Section, as it was shown in timetables, was always considered as a branch. The first stretch of 10 miles north from Aberdovey through the small village of Towyn to Llwyngwril was built in isolation. It opened in October 1863, three months after the main line had been extended from Machynlleth to Borth.

It was originally planned to make the junction with the coast line at Ynyslas on the opposite shore of the Dyfi from Aberdovey but the plan was abandoned because of the lack of firm foundations for a bridge across the river.

After Aberystwyth was rail-connected, further extension of the coast line lost momentum, partly because of a shortage of money — a factor which had dogged the whole of the Cambrian (and many Welsh railways) during construction. To encourage

fresh initiative, the company agreed in January 1865 to Savin's request to exercise its option to contribute £100,000, although paying only by instalments.

Construction of almost four miles north from Llwyngwril to Barmouth Junction was costly. Seamen joined navvies to carve a ledge in the face

of cliffs dropping down from Cader Idris. The ledge reached 86ft above the shore at Friog Rocks.

When track was laid to Barmouth Junction, on the south shore of the Mawddach estuary, in July 1865, Barmouth Viaduct was far from complete and it was not until 3 June 1867 that the viaduct, the longest in Wales, was hailed not only as a railway bridge, but also a tourist attraction. 'There is not such a Promenade Pier in Europe,' proclaimed the *Gossiping Guide*. 'The bridge is divided into two roads; one for trains and the other for trampers.' Its 113 spans were supported by over 500 timber piles and an iron section of eight spans, one of which could be dragged on wheels over the others. An opening span was necessary to maintain a right of way for ships to pass close to the northern shore of the estuary at Barmouth. While Friog was the most spectacular stretch of the coast line, Victorian visitors got the most sweeping carriage window views of sea and mountains as trains crossed the viaduct.

The Coast Section was linked to the main line on 14 August with the opening of the six miles between Aberdovey and Glandovey Junction (not called Dovey Junction until 1904). The section included four short tunnels near Aberdovey.

North of Barmouth, the coastal strip, dominated by Harlech Castle, was flatter but the railway builders had to bridge several fast-flowing estuaries, partly with timber pile embankments.

The longest construction stretch between Barmouth and Pwllheli was completed on 10 October 1867, when goods trains began using Barmouth Viaduct. Approaching Portmadoc, the line was taken across marshes about a quarter of a mile inland from the Traeth Mawr embankment — the Cob — used by the Festiniog Railway. It had been built to reclaim the tidal basin of the River Glaslyn. Opposition by the Festiniog Railway and local quarry owners defeated an A&WC attempt to build a branch to Festiniog. It was thrown out by Parliament in 1863 and nothing more was heard of it. Later, relations healed and an interchange station and sidings opened at Minffordd in 1872.

Portmadoc was the only intermediate place of any size between Barmouth and Pwllheli, where the terminus was about half a mile short of the town centre. This shortcoming was not rectified until summer 1907, when the line was extended across a new embankment forming part of a scheme to improve the sheltered inner harbour.

A new station replaced the original, which was then incorporated into that for goods. The Pwllheli extension was made in the wake of a number of moves to cross the Lleyn Peninsula to Porth Dinlleyn, which was named, though not shown as rail-linked, on Railway Clearing House maps of the period.

Pwllheli had been reached two years after the A&WC had been absorbed by the Cambrian — a move opposed by the LNWR and GWR. They

Cambrian Railways

Delightful Spring, Summer, and Winter Resorts.

ON THE SHORES OF
CARDIGAN BAY.

Magnificent Scenery. Bracing Air.

Safe Bathing and Boating. Fishing & all Outdoor Sports.

ABERYSTWYTH.

EXCELLENT GOLF LINKS.
RAIL and COACH TOURS
Through Unsurpassed Scenery.
HOLIDAY CONTRACT TICKETS.
Cheap Tickets between Coast Stations.

TOURIST, WEEK-END, and TEN DAYS' TICKETS issued to

Aberystwyth, Aberdovey, Barmouth, Borth, Criccieth, Dolgelley, Fairbourne, Harlech, Portmadoc, Pwllheli, Towyn, and the Spas of Mid Wales.

Express Trains, with through carriages, from the Principal Centres to the Cambrian Coast.

Guides, and full information at the L. & N. W. and G. W. London Offices. The Tourist Agencies of Messrs. Abraham Altham, Ltd.; Thos. Cook & Son; Dean & Dawson, Ltd.; Pickfords, Ltd.; Mr. Jno. Frame; and Mr. L. R. Stanton, or from the Superintendent of the Line, Oswestry.

S. WILLIAMSON,
General Manager.

OSWESTRY, 1914.

Above:
During the last summer of peace, 1914, the company advertised in tourist handbooks, the 'Delightful Spring, Summer and Winter resorts' of Cardigan Bay, *Author's collection*

sought running powers over the Coast Section when they joined it at Afon Wen and Dolgelley respectively within three years.

LNWR: Bangor-Afon Wen

From September 1867, the coast line was linked to the Chester & Holyhead main line by a 26-mile single branch from Menai Bridge, on the outskirts of Bangor. Savin constructed what was known as the Caernarvonshire Railway through almost empty countryside to Afon Wen, four miles east of Pwllheli, where the junction was almost as remote, and often as windswept, as Dovey Junction.

It was expected to become part of the Cambrian but the LNWR stepped in and acquired the new line in 1869.

Above:
A short embankment separated the north end of the main viaduct with a short, curved one spanning a tidal inlet. The locomotive is No 28 *Mazeppa*, one of four 2-4-0s bought from Sharp, Stewart in 1863 and seen after rebuilding 30 years later. *IAL/Bucknall Collection*

Below:
Barmouth Viaduct was built with an opening span to allow the passage of small coastal craft up and down stream. The original, ungainly draw-over structure was replaced some years later by a swinging span. *IAL*

Left:
Barmouth and No 28 *Mazeppa* again. The resort was a turn-round point for some local services to Machynlleth and Pwllheli.
A. G. Ellis/R. W. Miller collection

Centre left:
Cambrian 4-4-0s usually handled through trains. An unidentified locomotive heads a southbound train of mixed stock, including a horsebox behind the well-stocked tender.
A. G. Ellis/R. W. Miller collection

Below left:
A GWR coach with a roofboard has been attached to the rear of a northbound service, headed by 4-4-0 No 16, at Llanbedr & Pensarn. Llanbedr village was nearly a mile from the station.
IAL

Above right:
Six-wheel coaches were a common sight on local trains for many years. 4-4-0 No 16 on a northbound service in 1913. It survived the Grouping, not being scrapped until January 1925.
R. W. Miller collection

Right:
An unidentified 0-6-0, possibly No 45, which had a long life, surviving as GWR No 900 until 1945. It is heading a heavy wartime goods passing Llanbedr & Pensarn in 1917. *LGRP*

29

Left:
A Pwllheli-bound train approaches Harlech in the charge of 4-4-0 No 20. Passenger train timings were generous, almost 1½hr being allowed for the 36 miles from Machynlleth to Harlech, including nine intermediate stations. Five-minute stops were booked at Dovey Junction and Barmouth because of connections with other services.
R. W. Miller collection

Below:
Goods 0-6-0s were often used on local trains. No 18, seen leaving Harlech in 1911, passed third-hand to the Cambrian, having been part of Denbigh, Ruthin & Corwen Railway and LNWR stock. Built by Sharp, Stewart in 1875, it was not taken over by the GWR at Grouping.
H. W. Burman/
R. W. Miller collection

Coast line traffic was boosted after the opening by the GWR of a halt, which later became a station, at Penychain between Afon Wen and Pwllheli, in 1933, as construction began of a large holiday camp. It became a large naval training base during World War 2. Afterwards it was developed by Butlins and thousands of holidaymakers used either scheduled or special trains run on the Coast line and over the former LNWR branch between Afon Wen and the Chester & Holyhead main line at Menai Bridge. Former GWR 0-6-0 No 3209 departs with a Pwllheli-Barmouth service in 1961.
R. E. James-Robertson

Above:
Moat Lane. Besides a striking station with a large building which once housed a refreshment room, Moat Lane also had a small shed which attracted enthusiasts because of its allocation of veteran locomotives. In May 1938 W. A. Camwell found two Dean Goods 0-6-0s, Nos 2544 and 2545 and, in the yard, 0-6-0 No 880, ex-Cambrian 770, then within months of withdrawal; pannier tank No 2068, then working the Kerry branch; and 0-6-0 No 885, ex-Cambrian No 88. The Van branch engine — 0-6-0T No 819 — was also on shed. A GWR clerestory coach stands on the Mid-Wales line running north-south in the middle background.
W. A. Camwell/R. W. Miller Collection

Left:
Llanidloes on a dark and snowy Sunday 30 December 1962, where the farewell train, an SLS special, made a photo-stop. The Llanidloes & Newtown Railway headquarters building (left) was preserved after a public inquiry but the rest of the station and its layout, including the locomotive shed (right), have been replaced by the town bypass. *Author*

The Mid-Wales Railway

Compared with the main and coast lines, the Cambrian's third stem, the Mid-Wales Railway, was not quite as important. Its 48½ miles between Llanidloes and Talyllyn Junction, four miles from Brecon, were just 4¾ miles shorter than the coast line between Dovey Junction and Pwllheli.

It was renowned for its beauty, an Edwardian *Baddeley Guide* advising tourists: 'When, about two miles from Three Cocks, the engine whistles, be ready for a beautiful view in both directions as the train crosses the Wye at the foot of a horse-shoe bend.'

On a snowy day in December 1962, I heard some passengers on an SLS special, which ceremonially consigned most of the route to history, remarking on the beauty of the scenery. The oldest passenger was a man aged 102 who, at the age of four, had been taken by his mother to see the first train pass Pantydwr station.

The SLS special also formed the last train over the Hereford, Hay & Brecon, on a day when Brecon was wiped off the railway map with the simultaneous withdrawal of passenger services to Newport over the Brecon & Merthyr via Talyllyn Junction and Pant.

The MWR was born of the Manchester & Milford Mania scheme, whose promoters planned to branch from the MWR at Penpontbren near Llanidloes and tunnel under Plynlimon. The memorial to that remains some three miles of trackbed leading to the village of Llangurig.

The MWR was a monument to the achievements of Victorian engineers and surveyors, who reached a summit of 947ft above sea level at Pantydwr without a major engineering work. Construction through mostly empty countryside was protracted and after completion there was only one addition: an 1866 curve at Builth Road to the LNWR Central Wales line from Craven Arms to Llandovery. The LNWR took it over four years later.

Despite being a county town, Brecon grew very slowly: a quarter of a century after the Brecon &

Below:
After the original Mid-Wales Railway Talyllyn station closed to passengers in 1878, the modest building was converted into a private house — with goods sidings outside. *LPC*

Merthyr reached it in 1863 with a 19-mile single extension from Pant, the population was only 6,000.

The HH&B was unable to open a through route of 38½ miles from Hereford until the MWR completed the 7½ miles between Three Cocks and Talyllyn Junctions in September 1864 and it could exercise running powers for all traffic. Five years later the Midland began working the HH&B, which it went on to lease in 1874 and absorb in 1886, making it part of a through route to Swansea.

The Cambrian began working the MWR in 1888 but it was not until after the Victorian age had given way to the Edwardian that amalgamation took place in summer 1904. The MWR served so few places of any size that it was able to include them all on a large platform nameboard at Moat Lane: Llanidloes, Rhayader and Builth Wells. It had its critics, guidebooks warning passengers that they often had to wait for hours at Moat Lane for connections between the Mid-Wales and the Cambrian main line.

Above left:
Talyllyn Junction looking towards Brecon, with the Brecon & Merthyr approaching left and the Cambrian from Three Cocks Junction, right. Passenger services which called at Talyllyn Junction were lengthy: Moat Lane was 60 miles from Brecon; Newport 47 miles and Hereford 38 miles. *IAL*

Left:
Talgarth, some six miles east of Talyllyn Junction, was the destination of the Cambrian's last Royal train, when King George V unveiled the National War Memorial in July 1920. *LGRP*

Above right:
In July 1896, heavily decorated 4-4-0 No 63 waits at Llanidloes to work a Royal train from Moat Lane Junction to Talyllyn Junction.
R. W. Miller collection

Below right:
A less decorated Royal train of four-wheel carriages was run by the Cambrian over the Elan Valley Railway when King Edward VII opened Birmingham's waterworks in 1904. The Royal saloon is the second vehicle, with observation window. *LGRP*

Right:
Cambrian 2-4-0T No 58, which is known to have worked the Elan Valley line. Built by Sharp, Stewart in 1866, it is seen as rebuilt in 1894. It was one of three locomotives which formed the Cambrian's 'Seaham' class. Two, including No 58, survived until 1948.
IAL/Bucknall Collection

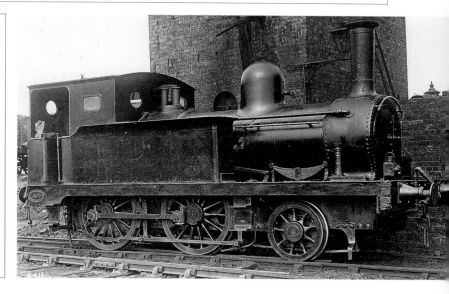

Mid Wales Railway

Proposed Booking Office & Waiting Room

for Shipwrens Station

Waiting Room

Office

Plan

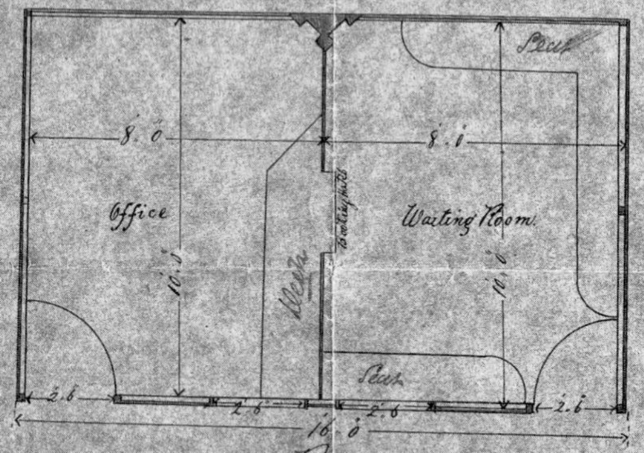

Scale ⅛ = Feet

Elevation

Left:
An original plan for a small booking office and waiting room at the remote Trefeinion station between Three Cocks and Talyllyn Junctions. It was sanctioned by the Cambrian board on 28 October and 11 November 1885.

Above:
The Mid-Wales Railway originally had 12 locomotives, including two Sharp, Stewart
0-6-0s identical to those of the Cambrian 'Queen' class. It included *Cambria*, seen at Machynlleth in the mid-1870s. *LPC*

Below:
No 2 — one of the MWR passenger fleet of six Kitson 0-4-2 tender locomotives — standing outside Builth Wells shed in the 1890s. It was the only MWR engine to retain its numberplate after Cambrian takeover. *IAL/Bucknall Collection*

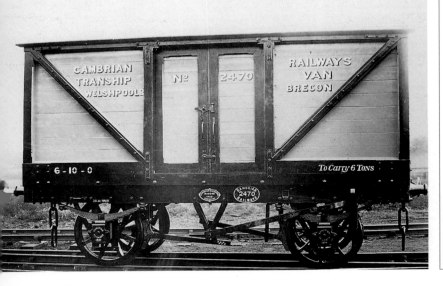

Left:
A heavy through working from Aberystwyth to Treherbert at Machynlleth, headed by 4-4-0 No 70 in August 1913. 0-6-0 No 91 stands on the down line. *LCGB*

Centre left:
Smoke from the tall chimneys of 'Beaconsfield' class 4-4-0s drifted across the Mid-Wales landscape for many years: An enthusiast in his eighties once wrote to me saying that although he could not remember seeing a Cambrian locomotive, he did have memories of seeing smoke trails of locomotives working on the Mid-Wales line. No 21 of the 'Beaconsfield' class was built by Sharp, Stewart in 1886 and not withdrawn until 1930. Another batch of the class was sold by the makers to the Furness Railway. *IAL/Bucknall Collection*

Below left:
A 6-ton capacity tranship van, for use between Welshpool and Brecon. Standard light grey and black-frame livery. *LCGB*

Right:
A 1913 August Bank Holiday cheap excursion from the West Midlands to South Wales was for a minimum of three days. It was organised by Thomas Cook and third class return fares to Talyllyn and Brecon both cost 10 shillings (50p).

MIDLAND

August Bank Holiday.

CHEAP EXCURSION TO SOUTH WALES.

ON SATURDAY, AUGUST 2nd,

COOK'S CHEAP EXCURSION TO

HEREFORD, HAY, TALYLLYN, BRECON,
NEATH & SWANSEA
(For the MUMBLES and GOWER)
(Via WORCESTER),

For 3, 4, 6, 7. 10. or 13 Days, will run as under:—

FROM					a.m.	FROM				p.m.
WALSALL	...	...	...	...	10†27	BIRMINGHAM (New Street)	...	...	1 12
Aldridge	...	...	...	...	10†35	Camp Hill	...	...	...	12†33
Sutton Coldfield	...	...	...	10†47	Moseley	...	...	...	12†31
				p.m.		King's Heath	...	...	...	12†28
Saltley	...	...	...	...	12†48	King's Norton	...	...	...	1*12

† Join Excursion Train at New Street.   * Via Barnt Green.

THIRD CLASS FARES THERE AND BACK.

To HEREFORD.	To HAY.	To TALYLLYN.	To BRECON.	To NEATH or SWANSEA.
6/6	**9/6**	**10/-**	**10/-**	**12/6**

RETURN ARRANGEMENTS.

On Monday, August 4th, Tuesday, August 5th, Thursday, August 7th, Friday, August 8th, Monday, August 11th, or Thursday, August 14th.

From	From	From
SWANSEA ...... 8.30 a.m. or 11. 5 a.m.	BRECON .... 10.30 a.m. or 1.10 p.m.	HAY .... 11.25 a.m. or 2. 9 p.m.
NEATH .... 8.25 a.m. or 11.20 a.m.	TALYLLYN ... 10.50 a.m. or 1.25 p.m.	HEREFORD ... 12.57 p.m. or 3.10 p.m.

CONDITIONS OF ISSUE OF TICKETS.

CHILDREN under three years of age, free; three years and under twelve, half-fares.

NOTICE.—The tickets are not transferable, and will be available only on the dates, by the trains, and at the stations named; if used on any other date, by any other train, or at any other station than those named, the tickets will be forfeited, and the full ordinary fare charged.

The Company give notice that tickets for this excursion are issued at a reduced rate, and subject to the condition that the Company shall not be liable for any loss, damage, injury, or delay to passengers, arising from any cause whatsoever. Sixty pounds of luggage allowed free at the owner's risk.

List of STATIONS, OFFICES, &c.,
OF THE
MIDLAND RAILWAY CO. and THOS. COOK & SON
WHERE TICKETS MAY BE OBTAINED.

MIDLAND RAILWAY CO.

WALSALL—The Station.
BIRMINGHAM—New St. Station; "Swan" Office, New St.; 46, Snow Hill; 1, George St., Parade; 44, Hall St.; and 3, Edgbaston St.
And at the OTHER STATIONS shewn herein.
Handbills can also be obtained at BIRMINGHAM at the Midland Parcels Receiving Offices in various parts of the town. TICKETS ISSUED ANY TIME IN ADVANCE.

, THOS. COOK & SON.

WALSALL—21, Park Street.
BIRMINGHAM—Stephenson Place; 52 and 54, Corporation Street; and 161, Soho Road.

MIDLAND FOLDERS, giving particulars of the Company's Services, Luggage, Parcels, &c., arrangements, may be had on application at any Midland Station or Agency.

The Midland Company's Illustrated Annual, "Country and Seaside Holidays," with Directory of Furnished Apartments in Country and Seaside Districts for 1913, may be obtained at Midland Stations and Bookstalls, &c.

Information with regard to the Company's arrangements can be obtained from the District Passenger Agent, Midland Railway, New Street Station, Birmingham.

Derby, July, 1913.

W.B. 124-1913. (5497.)

W. GUY GRANET, General Manager.

Thos. Cook & Son, Printers, London and Birmingham.

For Excursions to the WEST OF ENGLAND, see other Midland bills.

For Steamship Passenger Information, apply at Cook's Shipping, &c., Offices, Walsall and Birmingham.

Branches:
Standard and Narrow Gauge

The Cambrian is well remembered not only for the character of its main and coast lines and the often striking scenery through which they passed, but because of the individuality of its branches. No two were alike.

The first were built by the pioneer companies before they formed the Cambrian; others were constructed afterwards and some were developed privately. Besides those of standard gauge, there were two narrow gauge lines, both of which survive today.

Wrexham & Ellesmere

Two branches made strategically important connections with other railways: Barmouth Junction-Dolgelley, which joined the GWR Ruabon-Barmouth secondary route, and the nominally independent Wrexham & Ellesmere.

Later, the W&E was one of the last links in the Welsh Railway Union forged to establish a South Wales-Merseyside through route (reaching Liverpool via the Mersey Railway Tunnel) independent of the GWR and LNWR. It had a

complex history and was no match for the big companies. Neither was the hope realised that the Union would greatly increase goods traffic over the Cambrian and Mid-Wales Railways.

At Wrexham, the W&E joined the Great Central, which was soon to own the Wrexham, Mold & Connah's Quay Railway. Five years were allowed for completion when the 12¾ mile W&E was authorised in 1885 but it was not until a decade later (and two Acts for extension of time) that it opened, worked by the Cambrian. It was absorbed by the GWR at the Grouping. It ran through quiet, sparsely populated countryside, serving three small villages, to Wrexham Central where the station, far closer to the

Below:
A heavy goods departing Barmouth Junction for Dolgelley behind GWR No 884 (ex-Cambrian No 87 of 1899). A brake in the middle suggests the train will split for shunting at Dolgelley, where four sidings could accommodate 130 wagons. *A. G. Ellis*

town centre than that on the GWR Shrewsbury & Chester main line, was shared with the WM&CQ, together with exchange sidings. W&E local trains connected at Ellesmere with those on the Cambrian main line.

Barmouth Junction-Dolgelley

The single track branch of almost eight miles along the south bank of the Mawddach was more valuable to the GWR than to the Cambrian, because it gave Paddington access to the coast. It was built under powers obtained by the A&WC to blunt a determined GWR thrust through the Dee Valley to provide a much shorter route between the heavily populated areas of northwest England and Cardigan Bay than that via Machynlleth.

The GWR promoted five small companies to establish a 44-mile route from the Shrewsbury & Chester at Ruabon to Dolgelley. The Cambrian branch dated from 1865-9 and a short connecting extension at Dolgelley was completed by the nominally independent Bala & Dolgelley Railway the following year. The route gave the GWR its strongest presence in mid-Wales until it swallowed the Cambrian at Grouping.

The Dolgelley branch was charming, scenic and interesting because at Penmaenpool, where the track skirted a bend in the river, the Cambrian had a small engine shed and owned a toll bridge.

Early branches

The first three branches of what became the Cambrian Railways were authorised and built by the Oswestry & Newtown Railway. They were very different in character, serving industry and farming and a small but busy market town.

The Porthywaen branch

First to open in May 1861 was the Porthywaen branch, running 1¼ miles from the main line at Llynclys, four miles south of Oswestry, to expanding quarries. In Edwardian days its importance increased when it became the eastern stem of the Tanat Valley Light Railway (page 55).

Abermule-Kerry

Two years elapsed before the O&N opened the other two branches. The first goods train climbed from

Abermule to a small station and yard 550ft up in the Kerry Hills on the south side of the upper Severn Valley in March 1863. A sparse passenger service began the following July.

The impetus for the 3¾ mile branch came from a noted sheep breeder, who wanted the scattered farming and forestry community to share in the prosperity which the still incomplete Oswestry & Newtown was expected to bring. Farmers wanted to get sheep and produce to market quickly.

The climb from Abermule was steep, the single track being taken up the gorge of the River Mule at 1 in 43 for almost a mile. It was the steepest gradient on which the Cambrian operated passenger trains until the Welshpool & Llanfair opened in 1903. In *Forgotten Railways of North and Mid Wales*, written in the mid-1970s, I commended the branch as perfect for the meticulous modeller, especially as Dean 0-6-0s were among the last locomotives to use it. The thought remains valid today.

For about 30 years from 1888, the Kerry Hills echoed to the sound of steam from an extensive private 2ft gauge tramway. It was built to serve isolated farms and, more especially, extensive forestry plantations.

Llanfyllin branch

The 8½-mile line from Llanymynech to the market town of Llanfyllin was also built because of pressure from people living in small and isolated communities. Their leader was a local solicitor, John

Above:
The substantial station buildings at the terminus of the Kerry branch. The Cambrian branches had several remote terminals and Kerry lost its passenger service in 1931, although the branch sustained goods traffic for another quarter of a century. *LGRP*

Above right:
0-4-0ST No 36 *Plasfynnon* in a posed photograph with a mixed train at Kerry in 1904, when it was over 40 years old. The guard's van is standing on a short turntable. *LGRP*

Right:
Another view of a Kerry mixed train headed by *Plasfynnon* — with the fireman standing on the running board. The coach is No 84, built in Manchester in 1872. *IAL*

Pugh, grandfather of the locomotive engineer O. V. S. Bulleid, who lived in Llanfyllin as a boy.

For more than 30 years the branch layout at Llanymynech was chaotic and primitive. Through trains from Oswestry had to reverse twice as the line climbed steeply to cross the Shropshire Union Canal. It was not until 1896 that the branch approach to Llanymynech was improved by a short connection to the Llanymynech-Nantmawr branch of the Potteries, Shrewsbury & North Wales Railway. Besides radically improving operating, the connection cut journey times by 5-10min.

The Llanfyllin branch had an uneventful existence serving a large area of Montgomeryshire for nearly two decades, until it also became the railhead for construction by Liverpool Corporation of a reservoir and dam at Lake Vyrnwy, in the hills 10 miles away. When work began in summer 1881, 100 horses were stabled in the station yard to pull heavy construction materials on drays and wagons through steep and narrow lanes.

Occasionally the horses were harnessed to coaches carrying tourists whom the Cambrian encouraged to enjoy the area. Guidebooks suggested some might like to walk to the dam and back, but warned that there were no inns *en route*. There was plenty for tourists to see, for a five-mile long lake created when the reservoir opened in 1910 was one of the largest in Wales.

Llanymynech-Nantmawr

The PS&NWR — the famous 'Potts' — also reached the Nantmawr Quarries, completing a line from Shrewsbury (Abbey Foregate) in 1866. It crossed the O&N on the level at Llanymynech and passed under the Llanfyllin branch at Wern.

But the 'Potts' ran into interminable financial difficulties and at the request of a quarry owner, the Cambrian began working the four miles between Llanymynech and the quarries from 1881. This placed it in a strong position to refute attempts by

Col H. F. Stephens to reclaim the section after he revived the 'Potts' as the Shropshire & Montgomeryshire Light Railway in 1909. The Cambrian contended that it had worked the branch through years when there was no other company that could do it. The Nantmawr branch joined the Tanat Valley Light Railway, Blodwell Junction being created where it bisected the branch.

Aberdovey Harbour branch

A third branch completed in 1863 (besides those to Llanfyllin and Kerry) ran half a mile from the coast line at Aberdovey to the company-owned harbour. It pre-dated the Cambrian Railways, being authorised in 1861 by the A&WC and opened in October 1863, together with the 10-mile isolated section of the coast line north from Aberdovey to Llwyngwril.

The harbour grew into the Cambrian's biggest port. But it remained small, partly because railways quickly captured trade from coastal sailing ships. The harbour had cramped wharfs and sidings linked by small turntables which could handle only single wagons. But Aberdovey was noted for handling a wide variety of traffic, including foreign timber, and also construction materials for the Vyrnwy Dam.

The Van Railway

On 2 July 1896 the Cambrian got powers to work the Wrexham & Ellesmere Railway and also to run

Left:
Llanfyllin had a spacious layout for a branch serving a small town of under 2,000 inhabitants. The layout was at the end of an eight-mile single track, for which the Oswestry & Newtown Railway had got authorisation in 1861. R. W. Kidner describes it as 'Perhaps the least interesting of Cambrian branches'. *LGRP*

Right:
The Cambrian reopened and worked the Van branch in 1896 and among small locomotives it used in Edwardian days was its own 0-4-0ST No 22. This engine also occasionally worked the Kerry branch.
IAL/Bucknall Collection

over the Van Railway. Built under the Railways Construction Facilities Act of 1864, it ran 6½ miles from a small station close to the Cambrian's own at Caersws to lead mines at Van in the hills above the Severn Valley. Sixteen companies employed up to 1,000 people to work them, but only for a short time. The line opened for freight traffic in August 1871 and was improved to carry passengers under a Board of Trade Certificate of 1873.

Agreement with the Cambrian to maintain and work the line from 1896 ended a chequered spell which had lasted for years. Passenger traffic had been withdrawn in 1879 and the railway had closed entirely in 1893.

R. W. Kidner remarks in his Oakwood Press history of the Cambrian Railways, that when it reopened the line in 1896, the Cambrian was 'once again rushing in where angels had stubbed their

Above:
The Cambrian and Van Railways had separate passenger stations at Caersws. That of the Van closed to passengers in 1893 when services were withdrawn, but survived as a useful civil engineers' depot, incorporating the Van locomotive shed. It was used especially for bridge work. The building nearest the camera is modern. *LGRP*

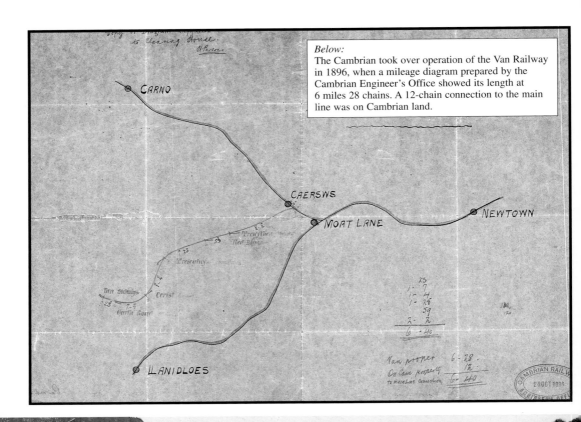

Below:
The Cambrian took over operation of the Van Railway in 1896, when a mileage diagram prepared by the Cambrian Engineer's Office showed its length at 6 miles 28 chains. A 12-chain connection to the main line was on Cambrian land.

THE
TANAT VALLEY LIGHT RAILWAY
IS NOW OPEN

giving access to some of the most charming river and mountain scenery in Wales, hitherto untrodden by the foot of the tourist.

The line, which is of standard gauge, leaves the Cambrian main line some 4 miles south of Oswestry, and, after running for 14 miles due west, terminates at Llangynog at the foot of the Berwyn Mountains, over 2,700 feet high.

The railway throughout its entire length traverses the valleys of the Tanat and Iwrch, both of which streams teem with trout and grayling.

It also affords the best access to Lake Vyrnwy (the Liverpool Corporation Waterworks reservoir), Penybontfawr Station being only 6 miles distant from the lake.

From Llanrhaiadr Mochnant, celebrated for its great pony fair, may be visited the great waterfall of Pistyll Rhaiadr, 4½ miles distant. The water descends in three falls a total distance of 240 feet, passing through a natural arch in its descent.

The whole district offers a most charming field for picnics, school outings, &c.

TOURIST TICKETS from Tanat Valley Stations to
ABERYSTWYTH, BARMOUTH, BUILTH, PWLLHELI. &c., &c.

Above:
The 1904 edition of *Baddeley's Tourist Guide* welcomed the new railway: 'It has greatly increased the accessibility of this interesting but comparatively little known part of the Principality for tourists — especially pedestrians... ' *Author's collection*

Below:
The Elan Valley Railway showing Cambrian 2-4-0T No 57 *Maglona* on a short goods train. From the Mid-Wales Railway, the Cambrian worked in and out of Noyadd Sidings built during the construction of Birmingham Corporation dams. *IAL/Bucknall collection*

Left:
During construction of four large dams in the Elan Valley between 1894-1917, Birmingham Corporation Waterworks built a private contractor's system of some seven miles. It stemmed from the Mid-Wales route at Noyadd, near Rhayader. An 0-6-0T pulls wagons near Garreg Ddu Viaduct. *Author's collection*

toes badly'. But passenger trains were reintroduced, though only running three times a week.

The Van Railway survived and the Cambrian secretary noted in an internal memorandum that under its agreement, the rent was reduced from £100 per annum to £80 from 1 January 1914. During World War 1 — when the mines were still open under government control — the branch also handled timber from local forests. The mines, with lead seams up to 900ft deep, finally closed in 1920 but their legacy of spoil heaps was a rich one for the Cambrian, being a source of ballast, valuable because of weed-killing properties.

The story of the Van was well told in a paperback guide of that title published in 1953 by a Londoner, Lewis Cozens. His record is particularly valuable because he drew upon the memories of a number of Welsh people who knew the line.

Elan Valley Railway

The Elan Valley Railway (1894-1917) was not strictly part of the Cambrian story because it was private. Mostly constructed by a large contractor, Lovatt of Wolverhampton, it was operated by Birmingham Corporation Waterworks Department as it built four large dams. They supply water to the city through an aqueduct more than 70 miles long.

The line, which extended several miles into the hills flanking the Severn Valley, left the Mid-Wales Railway through a junction built about half a mile south of Rhayader. A loop was built on the main line and Noyadd sidings for the exchange of traffic with the Cambrian were constructed close by.

About the time the first stretch of line was completed in 1894, the Corporation rejected an approach from the Cambrian to work the line but it was agreed that the Cambrian should work construction traffic to the site of Caban Coch Dam, about three miles from Elan Junction.

In the 1960s, the Mid-Wales again carried dam construction traffic when the large Clywedog Dam was built in the hills above Llanidloes. The eight-mile northern tip of the Mid-Wales Railway between there and Moat Lane was retained until October 1967 for cement traffic from South Wales. The only route was via Shrewsbury.

Light Railways

Nowhere was the diversity of the Cambrian Railways more evident than in the working, rather than ownership, of three rural branches built in the

---

Below:
The Tanat Valley timetable incorporated a sparse connecting service over the 2½-mile branch between Blodwell Junction and Llanymynech, where 0-6-0 No 15 heads a train composed of six-wheel brake third No 78, built 1901, and four-wheel composite No 81, built 1864, forming a through working to Llangynog. *LGRP*

Above:
A classic W. A. Camwell study of the 1930s, with ex-Cambrian 2-4-0T No 1197 heading a train of mixed LMS, GWR and private wagons away from Llangynog.
W. A. Camwell

Below:
The Tanat scene in 1930. The generally sparse nature of passenger traffic is emphasised by two small coaches (with double running boards) being sufficient for a train from Llangynog to Oswestry. *LGRP*

wake of the Light Railways Act of 1896 and completed between 1902 and 1904. The Vale of Rheidol, Welshpool & Llanfair and standard gauge Tanat Valley were built by independent companies.

The Tanat Valley Light Railway

The TVLR made the deepest penetration of the lightly populated valleys of the Welsh border country, stemming from the Nantmawr Quarry branch. Authorised in 1899, the Light Railway ran 14 miles from Porthywaen up the steadily narrowing valley to the lead mining village of Llangynog at the foot of the Berwyn Mountains.

Above left:
A Llangynog train at Blodwell Junction in 1904, with rebuilt 2-4-0T No 58. A four-wheel first/second class composite is marshalled between third class compartment stock. *LGRP*

Below left:
Blodwell Junction, where working timetables stated complicated rules for passing passenger and goods trains. The Tanat Valley branch headed west on a gentle right-hand curve after passing the junction of the Llanymynech branch, which turned south. *LGRP*

Below:
Llangedwyn, approximately halfway between Oswestry and Llangynog. Rather a spacious station for so remote a rural district. *LGRP*

The section from Blodwell was over the course of the proposed 'Potts' line intended to link the district with Shrewsbury. A *Baddeley Tourist Guide* published when the Tanat Valley opened, noted that a pub at Pen-y-Bont, called The Railway Inn to record the 'Potts' scheme, took 20 years to justify its name.

Like the Welshpool & Llanfair, the Tanat was constructed by John Strachan, a Cardiff contractor. No major engineering works were needed. Blodwell Junction, six miles from Oswestry, occupied the site of the 'Potts' Llanyblodwell station, and was the only place where the Cambrian had running powers in opposite directions over a neighbouring company — the Shropshire Railways to Llanymynech for all traffic (2 miles 36 chains) and from Blodwell to Nantmawr for merchandise (1 mile 31 chains).

The pattern of Tanat passenger services introduced by the Cambrian when the branch opened in January 1904 brought a new way of life to many people living in the valley who could now leave in the morning to work in Oswestry and return in the evening. Small tank locomotives of pensionable age adequately handled a couple of four-wheel compartment coaches forming four weekday services each way, some mixed. The first left Llangynog about 7am and, having called at 10 intermediate stations, reached Oswestry about 75min later; the last returned from Oswestry in early evening. There were no part-way services.

The Tanat Valley, its railway and industries, found a noted historian in Dr W. J. Wren whose David &

Charles book has helped to keep memories alive and encouraged modellers to recapture the special atmosphere of remote Cambrian branches.

The Welshpool & Llanfair Light Railway

It is perhaps remarkable that *both* Cambrian-associated narrow gauge lines — the W&L and the Vale of Rheidol — should have survived the Beeching axe and flourish to the delight not only of enthusiasts, but also tourists and holidaymakers who travel simply for enjoyment.

Both were built for passengers and goods, although the Llanfair was notable as the only Welsh narrow gauge line built without the impetus of mineral traffic. Rather it was to be a lifeline for scattered farming communities centred on the little town of Llanfair Caereinion, nine miles west of Welshpool. Schemes for a line between the mainly agricultural towns were current from the early 1860s until the Light Railways Act led to the building of the route that is today in the care of enthusiasts. A gauge of 2ft 6in was chosen as being the best for conquering the rolling hills, allowing for sharp curves and stiff gradients. A 1,738yd climb of 1 in 29 through the Pass of Golfa near Welshpool displaced the 1 in 43 ascent on the Kerry branch as the steepest on which the Cambrian worked passenger services.

An even greater obstacle was taking the track through a congested built-up area of Welshpool. The solution was to lay it over part of an old tramway and carry it on a platform over the Sylfaen Brook.

The Light Railway company remained independent until it was absorbed by the GWR on 1 January 1923. But it was always regarded locally as Cambrian, which was shown as the owning company in *Bradshaw's* for many years.

The Vale of Rheidol Light Railway

The VOR gauge of 1ft 11⅝in was narrower than several others, including the Corris and Talyllyn, because its sinuous route involved curves of only three chains radius.

The company was formed after an inquiry by the Light Railway Commissioners. An Act, not a Light Railway Order, was obtained in August 1897 for a 12-mile line from Aberystwyth Harbour and a passenger terminus near that of the Cambrian, to Devil's Bridge. Construction started from the harbour in 1900, with materials brought in by sea. When traffic on the Plynlimon & Hafan Tramway ceased in 1899 — after only three precarious years — the VOR contractor bought materials and also a locomotive and wagons, which were regauged from 2ft 3in.

The VOR opened to passengers in Christmas week 1902. It climbed from 14ft at the coast to 680ft at Devil's Bridge — just 13ft short of the height of Talerddig summit. The maximum gradient was 1 in 48 and because so much of the route was cut into the side of a hill overlooking the Vale, passengers were advised to sit on the left hand side. Guides warned the first tourists that parts of the Rheidol Valley were 'greatly disfigured by industrial works'. These were ore mines, some of which were connected to the railway by aerial ropeways.

During the delay between the authorisation and start of construction, hopes were high that the VOR would be extended 16 miles along the cliffs south of Aberystwyth to the small fishing village of Aberayron. An Extension Order was obtained in August 1898, but construction was never started, despite fresh powers being granted in 1909.

One unanswered question is whether the Cambrian would have benefited had VOR trains run

Above:
The last of the Cambrian's narrow gauge acquisitions, which took place in 1913, was of the Vale of Rheidol, which had opened 11 years earlier. From 14ft at Aberystwyth, it climbs to 680ft at Devil's Bridge, on a maximum gradient of 1 in 48. Two tall signals controlling the loop were the most prominent features at Aberffrwd. *National Library of Wales/R. W. Miller Collection*

Above right:
Vale of Rheidol departure from Aberystwyth behind 2-4-0T *Rheidol*, bought secondhand from the Hafan & Talybont Tramway and rebuilt from 2ft 3in to the VoR's 1ft 11¾ in gauge. *IAL/Bucknall Collection*

Right:
Festiniog saddle tank *Palmerston* departing Aberystwyth in summer 1913, while on loan to the VoR. *LCGB*

into its station at Aberystwyth. The probable answer is no, because the Cambrian never sought to make the switch, even after the VOR amalgamated with it in 1913. It was left to the GWR to make the short extension after the Grouping.

The Mawddwy Railway

Part of the fascination of old *Bradshaw's* lies in studying single pages crammed with timetables of several companies. Typical was page 193 of the July 1885 summer issue, which included the Mid-Wales and two of the other three lines serving Brecon; plus the Talyllyn (which it is always pleasant to recall

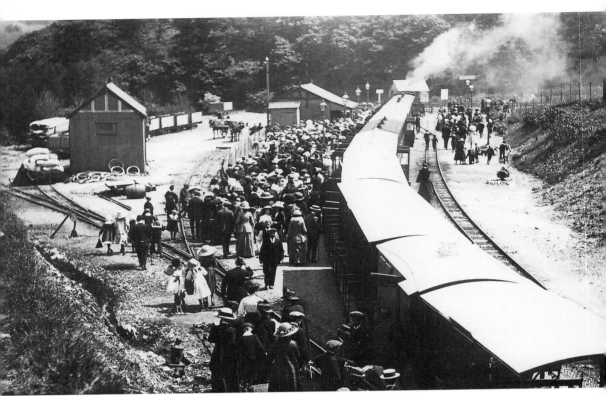

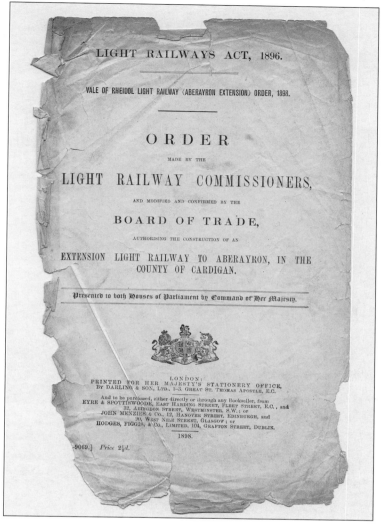

when thinking of the Cambrian), and the Mawddwy Railway. It flitted in and out of *Bradshaw's* as its fortunes ebbed and flowed.

It was built privately and opened in 1867, from the Newtown & Machynlleth at Cemmes Road to the village of Dinas Mawddwy, a route of nearly seven miles which had been surveyed by the Cambrian's engineer, George Owen. Twelve years after the smoke of the Mawddwy's two 0-6-0 Manning Wardle saddle tanks first animated the lonely and remote Upper Dovey Valley, the author of a *Gossiping Guide to Wales* wondered if Dinas Mawddwy might be the most unlikely place in Britain to find a railway station.

That station had an impressive stone gateway (still standing in 1998), despite being half a mile short of the village. It was first removed from passenger timetables in 1901. Goods continued

until 1908, when the railway closed completely. Yet only three years later, it reopened as a Light Railway with the support of local authorities, being worked by the Cambrian.

The line carried a variety of timber and mineral traffic and slate from quarries including the Hendre-Ddu, which had its own narrow gauge tramway system of some six miles.

Bus competition led the GWR to withdraw passenger services on New Year's Eve 1930 but more than a decade later, in March 1943, the GWR Sectional Appendix warned staff that 'Mawddwy Branch Train' passengers must not be allowed to remain in the train while it was being transferred between the main line and the branch. Such movements — if they still took place — were impossible after summer 1951, when the branch was closed completely by the Western Region.

Left:
Although it tried hard to attract tourists, the Mawddwy Railway's main passenger traffic was local. Dinas Mawddwy terminus about 1900, with 0-6-0ST *Mawddwy* heading a train for Cemmes Road. *R. W. Miller collection*

Below left:
Mixed train at Dinas Mawddwy headed by GWR No 1329. Built by the GWR at Wolverhampton in 1883 and rebuilt in 1906, the 2-4-0 at one time carried the Cambrian numberplate No 1. *IAL/Bucknall Collection*

Above right:
Mawddwy at Cemmes Road about the turn of the century. Coach No 4, behind the engine, has individual compartments for three classes. The other coach, No 5, is a third brake. All Mawddwy coaches were scrapped when the Cambrian took over in 1911. *Mawddwy* was rebuilt and transferred to the Van Railway, where it worked through the GWR years until closure in 1940. *IAL/Bucknall Collection*

Centre right:
Summer morning arrival at Machynlleth from Dinas Mawddwy in 1913, in the charge of Cambrian 2-4-0 No 53. The tall wooden signalbox has its nearest wall weather-protected. *LCGB*

Below right:
Machynlleth station of the narrow gauge Corris Railway, after rebuilding in 1910. After Nationalisation, control of the station passed to the stationmaster at the main line station. *IAL*

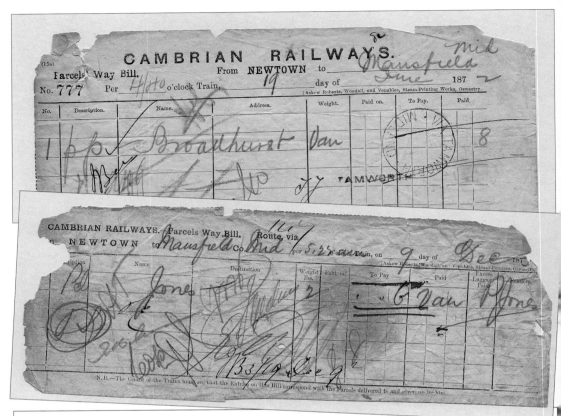

CAMBRIAN RAILWAYS.

Parcels Way Bill, From NEWTOWN to _Mansfield mid_

No. 777 Per 4/40 o'clock Train, _19_ day of _June_ 187_2_

[Askew Roberts, Woodall, and Venables, Steam-Printing Works, Oswestry.]

No.	Description.	Name.	Address.	Weight.	Paid on.	To Pay.	Paid.
1	p p	_Broadhurst Van_					8
		TAMWORTH					

CAMBRIAN RAILWAYS. Parcels Way Bill. Route, via

NEWTOWN to _Mansfield Co Mid_ per _5.29_ o'clock Train, on _9_ day of _Dec_ 187_

[Askew Roberts, Woodall an' Venables, Steam-Printers, Oswestry.]

...ption	Name	Destination	Weight lbs.	Paid on.	To Pay	Paid	Excess Luggage Paid	...nders
Pc	_Jones_				_C Van_			_P Jones_

N.B.—The Guard of the Trains must see that the Entries on this Bill correspond with the Parcels delivered to and given up by him.

Top:
A parcel sent from Newtown to Mansfield (Midland) by the 4.40pm train on 19 June 1872 was routed via Tamworth (Midland).

Above:
A parcels way bill for a consignment sent on the 5.29pm train from Newtown to Mansfield on 9 December 1870. The parcel was routed via Tamworth (Midland). The way bill instructed guards to see that entries on it corresponded with parcels handled. *Author's collection*

Below:
The Cambrian was ever publicity-conscious and in the early Edwardian era took the first complete train it built at Oswestry to Llanymynech to have it photographed. The rake of coaches was mixed and so was the locomotive, in the sense that its tender was borrowed, as the one it was to have was still being built. *R. W. Miller collection*

Below right:
The Cambrian helped Aberdovey to grow as a charming resort and as its busiest port, which was served by a short branch off the coast line. It is being shunted by 0-6-0 No 46. *IAL*

Bankruptcy and Growth

Uniting the companies which built the main and coast lines brought disunity, though it was never serious enough to affect growth. The first major development, moving the headquarters to Oswestry in 1866, failed to assuage disagreements between the directors of the inland section and those nominated to represent the interests of the coast section.

Cambrian finances were fragile for years, not least because it twice went bankrupt. The first occasion, in 1868, ended when the inland and coast directors agreed to share net profits. A decade later, soon after the board had been reconstructed, David Davies, a pioneer of railways and a Cambrian director, criticised it publicly. He claimed it was not a safe railway and would soon be sprinkled with human blood.

The attack was soon forgotten, but finance remained a crucial concern and when receipts fell, action by bankers placed the railway in Chancery in summer 1884. The directors became managers and John Conacher, the secretary, became the receiver. He was an able administrator and after only a few months a financial reorganisation scheme was accepted by creditors and the company discharged from bankruptcy.

At almost the same time, a general trade depression, which had particularly affected the Welsh slate industry and added to the Cambrian's troubles, eased. Then came a decade in which the Cambrian was transformed from little more than a long rural branch into a main line railway.

The strongest build-up was in passenger revenues, which rose from £86,000 in 1893 to £110,000 in 1903. Those for goods, minerals and cattle, generally smaller, increased from only £54,000 in 1893 to £76,000 10 years later.

Not all initiatives were successful. The 1890s saw the collapse of a scheme of 1889 to introduce shipping services, based on Aberdovey, the nearest port to the Midlands. Parliamentary assent to provide or build steamers and work, let and use them between Aberystwyth, Aberdovey, Portmadoc and Pwllheli, and the Irish ports of Wexford, Rosslare, Waterford, Wicklow and Arklow, was strongly opposed by Dublin steamboat owners and major railway companies, notably the LNWR, which operated Irish cross-Channel services from

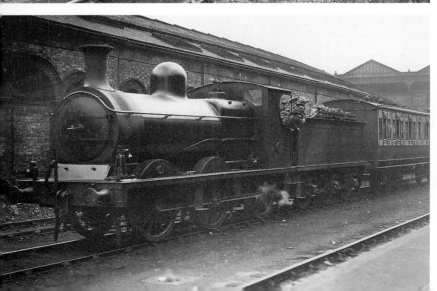

Left:
Arriving at Welshpool: an express headed by 4-4-0 No 66 with four horseboxes leading. Public timetables included a footnote that horseboxes and carriage trucks were only conveyed by stated trains between certain points, 'particulars of which can be ascertained from the stationmasters'.
R. W. Miller collection

Centre left:
Because little industry developed in mid-Wales, passenger services always formed the backbone of the Cambrian traffic. One notable speed-up took place in 1891, especially services between Whitchurch and Aberystwyth. A number of Sharp, Stewart 4-4-0s were introduced over the next few years. No 67 dated from spring 1893. *IAL/Bucknall Collection*

Below left:
The Cambrian had a minor presence at Crewe, where its locomotives which worked-in over the Shrewsbury & Crewe line from Whitchurch, were serviced at North Shed. No 54 was one of several types of Cambrian 0-6-0s which added diversity and interest to the Crewe scene before Grouping.
R. W. Miller collection

Above right:
An 'urgent' goods wagon dispatch label from 1894, Oswestry to Whitchurch.

Below right:
The Cambrian worked several Royal trains through the years. Probably the most important occasion was during an official State Visit for the Investiture of the Prince of Wales at Caernarvon in June 1911. 4-4-0s Nos 83 and 81 leave Harlech with the LNWR Royal stock. Many special trains ran to Caernarvon, several handled by Cambrian locomotives, which worked through over the LNWR branch via Afon Wen.
R. W. Miller collection

Holyhead. The Cambrian introduced two small paddle steamers on a service between Aberdovey and Waterford. But it was abandoned after only a few months, when rival companies threatened to cut rates below economic limits. However, Aberdovey thrived and remained the Cambrian's busiest port, exporting slate and importing a variety of materials, including sleepers.

In February 1901, only weeks after the death of Queen Victoria, takeover was in the air when shareholders considered a motion to see if the LNWR, Midland or GWR (in that order) would be interested in buying the company. Only two Cambrian directors voted in favour.

The Cambrian finally became a successful railway when the Victorians and Edwardians of all social classes began to travel widely and enjoy holidays. It had been trying for years to exploit the attractions of Cardigan Bay, for people living in the crowded towns and cities of Lancashire and Merseyside, Birmingham and the Black Country, who were able to reach the coast on day trips as well as holidays. The Cambrian had a monopoly on rail traffic from those areas to Aberystwyth but it competed with the GWR as Barmouth grew into an attractive resort, even though the western tip of the route from Dolgelley was over the Cambrian. Edwardian Guides warned that lodgings at Barmouth were in 'great request' during August and September when prices were high. The Cambrian also competed with the GWR for traffic from South Wales to Aberystwyth.

The Cambrian issued weekend and 10-day tickets throughout the year to a host of 'watering places': Aberystwyth, Borth, Aberdovey, Towyn, Dolgelley, Llanbedr & Pensarn, Harlech, Barmouth,

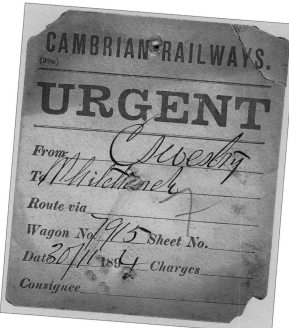

Portmadoc, Criccieth and Pwllheli (for Nevin). They were resorts and places to which Cambrian publicity booklets stated that the LNWR and GWR issued weekend tickets from London stations.

Enterprise was not restricted to trying to attract day trippers and holidaymakers. It encouraged the wealthy to build summer residences at watering places by offering free five-year passes to the heads of families who built and occupied houses with an annual rental of not less than £50. Plans had to be approved by the Company's engineer.

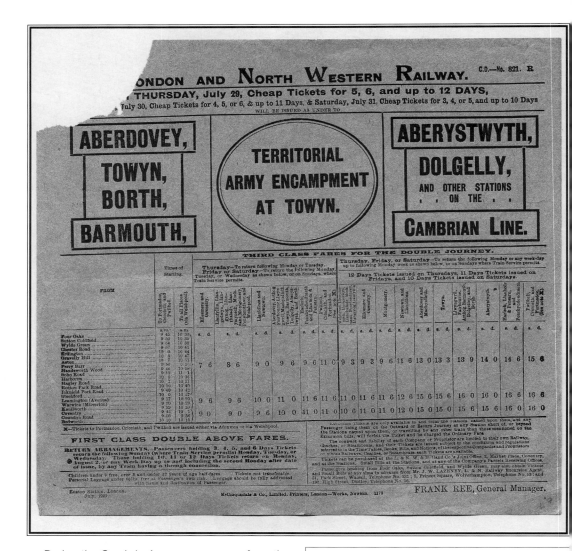

During the Cambrian's summer season from the beginning of May to the end of October, a variety of reduced fares and rates were offered. They included rates for the carriage of linen boxes, hampers and vegetables for tourists staying with their families on the coast. Golfers could buy cheap day returns for playing on 'links' at Pwllheli, Harlech, Barmouth, Aberdovey, Borth and Fairbourne, while passengers wanting to shoot and fish within easy reach of many stations could have their enquiries 'answered by station masters'.

Included in the Mid-Wales Railway Amalgamation Bill of 1903 was a scheme to provide feeder services with motorbuses. The first, not launched until three years later, was over a 10-mile route from Pwllheli to small villages in the Lleyn Peninsula. It grew to five weekday services by 1913, but was never a success.

Above:
Large Territorial Army camps were held at several places along the coast, mainly in the Aberystwyth and Towyn areas, and the LNWR was among companies which encouraged wives and children to visit the men while they were living under canvas. In July 1909, passengers were allowed to carry up to 60lb of personal luggage free.

The Cambrian closely studied the growth of motorbus and coach competition as became evident from an internal engineer's office memo of 1905. It showed distances by road to Aberystwyth from 24 towns in North, Mid and South Wales and just three across the Border: Chester (98¾ miles), Shrewsbury (76) and Oswestry (71¾).

'The Sun is your Host on the Cambrian Coast.' This catchy motto was that of the Cambrian Resorts

Association, formed in 1909 and based at Barmouth, with senior Cambrian officers as the first two company secretaries. Soon afterwards, the Coast got a tremendous boost, not from tourist promotion but from the War Office, which chose the Coast and notably the Aberystwyth area as the site for tented Territorial Army camps, where men trained in their thousands.

In 1912, as war clouds gathered in Europe, 4½ miles of the main line between Newtown and Moat Lane were doubled. The improved section was tested to capacity one summer Sunday, when 13,000 troops and 800 horses were carried. By the time peace returned in 1918, the Cambrian had carried some 250,000 troops and their equipment.

During the war, people living near the Mid-Wales Railway were disturbed night and day by trains blasting up the steep banks, carrying thousands of tons of coal a week from South Wales to the Grand Fleet of the Royal Navy. It was based at Scapa Flow, but the trains ran only to Grangemouth.

As life returned to normal after the war, the *LNWR Guide to Health Resorts* promoted the attractions of Aberystwyth and surrounding areas. Yet it listed only a single furnished lodging to let. It was a boarding house 400yd from the station, owned by a woman 'late of Birmingham'. The Cambrian did better, advertising 'combined Railway and Hotel Weekend' tickets from all over England to four hotels at Aberystwyth and others at seven other destinations.

In the years before World War 1, the company's steady, rather than spectacular, growth was reflected by traffic receipts. In 1907, they totalled £326,000. In 1913, they reached £357,000. In neither year was any dividend paid on ordinary stock.

Above right:
Harlech Music Festival: a 1913 handbill.

Right:
Also photographed at Harlech by H. W. Burman, who took many shots on the Cambrian, was the Royal staff support train for the 1911 visit, headed by 4-4-0 No 11, the second locomotive to be built at Oswestry Works. A member of Aston's '61' class, it was completed in 1904.
H. W. Burman/
R. W. Miller collection

CAMBRIAN RAILWAYS.

TOURS IN WALES.

Bathing, Boating, Fishing (Sea, River, and Lake), Golfing, Coaching, Mountaineering.

TOURIST TICKETS available for two months, issued throughout the year from London and all principal Stations in England, Scotland, and Ireland, to
Aberystwyth, Bor'th, Machynlleth, Aberdovey, Towyn, Dolgelley, Barmouth, Harlech, Llanbedr, Pensarn, Portmadoc, Criccieth, Pwllheli, Llanidloes, Rhayader, Builth Wells and **Brecon.**

CHEAP WEEK-END AND TEN DAYS TICKETS

are issued every Friday or Saturday **THROUGHOUT THE YEAR** from SHREWSBURY, BIRMINGHAM, WOLVERHAMPTON. STAFFORD, BURTON, DERBY, LEICESTER, LEEDS, HUDDERSFIELD, STOCKPORT, OLDHAM, MANCHESTER, PRESTON, BLACKBURN, ROCHDALE, BRADFORD, WAKEFIELD, HALIFAX, BOLTON, WIGAN, WARRINGTON, CREWE, LIVERPOOL, STOKE, BIRKENHEAD, and Other Stations to the CAMBRIAN WATERING PLACES.

Commencing on June 1st, and on **Every Wednesday** in June, July, August, and September up to September 21st, Cheap Weekly and Fortnightly Tickets will be issued from **London** to the Cambrian Coast and certain inland stations, **available to Return** on the following Monday or Thursday, or on the Monday week, or Thursday fortnight. Tickets at same Fares are also issued during the same period (June 2nd to September 22nd) on Every Thursday **To London,** available to return following Wednesday, or Wednesday week.

ABOUT 30 RAIL AND COACH EXCURSIONS DAILY,

Are run from the Cambrian Railways during the Summer Months, through the finest scenery in the Principality. Cycling and Walking Tours at cheap fares throughout the Mountain, River and Lake District of North and Mid Wales. For particulars see Rail and Coach Excursions Programme, issued gratis.

Express Trains with 1st and 3rd Class Lavatory Carriages Lighted with Gas.

(LONDON TO ABERYSTWYTH 6¾ HOURS, BARMOUTH 7¼)

Are run daily during the Season in connection with Fast Trains on the London and North Western and other Railways, between London, Liverpool, Manchester, Birmingham, Stafford, Shrewsbury, Hereford, Merthyr, Cardiff, Newport (Mon.), &c., and Aberystwyth, Barmouth, &c.

SEE THE CAMBRIAN RAILWAYS NEW AND BEAUTIFUL ALBUM "A SOUVENIR,"

GEMS OF PICTURESQUE SCENERY IN WILD WALES.

55 Superb Views. Price 6d.

At the principal Railway Bookstalls, the Company's Stations and the undermentioned Offices, &c.

"PICTURESQUE WALES" (Illustrated.)

The Official Guide Book to the Cambrian Railways, edited by Mr. GODFREY TURNER, price 6d., can be obtained at the Bookstalls, and at the Company's Offices or Stations, also of Messrs. W. J. Adams & Sons, 59, Fleet-street, London, E.C.

Farm House and Country Lodgings.—Attention is drawn to the revised illustrated Pamphlet issued by the Company. "**WHERE TO STAY AND WHAT TO SEE,**" Price 1d., at the principal Railway Bookstalls and Company's Stations.

Time Tables, Tourist Programmes, Guide Books, and full particulars of Trains, Fares, &c., may be obtained from Mr. W. H. GOUGH, Superintendent of the Line, Oswestry, at any of the Company's Stations, and at the Cambrian Office, Crue-Woode Buildings, 17, Back Goree, LIVERPOOL, or on application to the undersigned. Also at the Cambrian Railway's Company's London Offices, 153, Fenchurch Street, E.C., 18, Cockspur Street, S.W., and 11, Onslow Place, S.W., and at the undermentioned Offices of Messrs. Henry Gaze & Sons, Ltd., Excursion Tourist Agents—
LONDON—142, Strand, 4, Northumberland Avenue, 18, Westbourne Grove, and Piccadilly Circus; BIRMINGHAM—Stephenson Place, New Street Station; MANCHESTER—L. & N.W. Booking Office, London Road; LIVERPOOL—25, Lime Street; DUBLIN—16, Suffolk Street; GLASGOW—Central Station.

General Offices,   **C. S. DENNISS,**
Oswestry, 1898.   **General Manager.**

Above:
Considering the beauty of the coast, it is perhaps surprising that the Cambrian did not run more observation coaches. This conversion from two coaches ran between Pwllheli and Machynlleth. *LGRP*

Right:
Tourist information booklets like that for the first half of the 1905 summer season, were not confined to attracting holidaymakers from major centres of population, including the West Midlands and the Lancashire 'Watering Places', to mid-Wales; they also detailed 'reverse direction' weekend tickets for local people to travel widely in England and Scotland.

CAMBRIAN RAILWAYS
Tourist Arrangements

C.S. DENNISS.
SECRETARY. & GEN. MANAGER.

1905 May 1st to June. 30th

CAMBRIAN RAILWAYS,

FOR PICTURESQUE WALES

VIA **THE LONDON & NORTH WESTERN,**
AND VIA **THE GREAT WESTERN**

RAILWAYS IN DIRECT
CONNECTION WITH ALL
STATIONS ON THE

SOUTH EASTERN AND CHATHAM

RAILWAY;

ALSO WITH THE
CONTINENT.

✻❁✻

THIRTY
Rail and
Coach
Trips
Daily.

ABERYSTWYTH.
*(From a photograph
by Mr. E. R. Gyde,
Aberystwyth.)*

TOURIST
TICKETS
are issued to the
Cambrian Coast
from all the principal
Stations in the Country
all the year round.

SNOWDON AND
CRIB-GOCH.
*(From a photo-
graph by
Mr. I. Slater,
Llandudno.)*

WEEK END AND
TEN DAYS
TICKETS.
are also issued every Friday
and Saturday to all the principal
Stations on the Cambrian Line.

✻❁✻

C. S. DENNISS,
Secretary and General Manager.

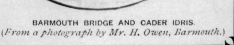

BARMOUTH BRIDGE AND CADER IDRIS.
(From a photograph by Mr. H. Owen, Barmouth.)

Working the Line

Management and men

The Cambrian had a profound effect on the economy of Wales, providing employment for people living in remote, thinly populated country districts. It also stopped them having to leave their families to find jobs in distant, fast growing towns and cities.

A job on the railway was regarded by many as one for life. While it never offered job security, the Cambrian did provide some welfare facilities. A friendly society was formed as early as 1865 and although not subsidised by the company, it gave sickness, accident and death benefits to all grades, although there were no superannuation, widow's pension or child allowance schemes.

Some ambitious men left to seek promotion in bigger companies in Britain, Ireland and North America, a notable move being that of George Findlay, who resigned from management in 1865 to become general goods manager of the LNWR.

Some men who had joined the Cambrian as boys a decade or more before Grouping went on to work for the GWR for more years than they did for the Cambrian.

The insensitive handling of staff after a minor accident at Ellesmere station in 1891 led to a significant improvement in working conditions of railwaymen throughout Britain. It was one of the few occasions when the Cambrian made national news.

The Hood Case, as it became known, began when a porter named Humphries was accused of slackness after a mail train was derailed because he reached a ground frame too late to set the road correctly. He was sacked after the directors rejected his excuse of being tired through working excessive hours. The board was furious when the stationmaster, John Hood, signed a memorandum calling for Humphries' reinstatement, and demoted him to be in charge at Montgomery, a little-used station which timetables warned was nearly two miles from the pretty, hill-top village. Subsequently, Hood was sacked after giving evidence to a Select Committee which the House of Commons had recently set up to investigate the excessive hours worked by railwaymen.

His case was taken up by the Amalgamated Society of Railway Servants and a Breach of Parliamentary Privilege was established after MPs decided Hood had been censured in a manner likely to deter other railway servants from giving evidence before the Committee. The Government, led by Gladstone as Prime Minister, advocated the House accepting an apology by several Cambrian directors called before it, but they were found guilty of a

Left:
In 1908, the Cambrian tried hard to attract tourists to 'Picturesque Wales'. In the South Eastern & Chatham Official Guide, a Cambrian advertisement, which embraced Snowdonia as well as the coast, told readers they could get to Cardigan Bay via the LNWR and GWR.

Right:
The first locomotives that ran through the Severn Valley had open footplates. *Wynnstay*, which became Cambrian No 4, was delivered by Sharp, Stewart in 1859 — the year the Llanidloes & Newtown Railway opened. Later it also worked on the Oswestry & Newtown, opened the following year. It was one of a class of six 0-4-2 locomotives. The last was withdrawn in 1899.
IAL/Bucknall Collection

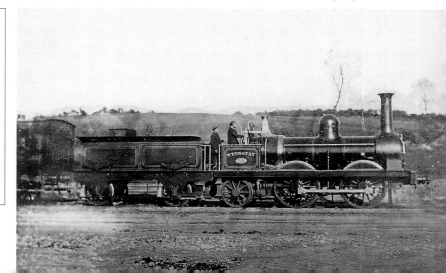

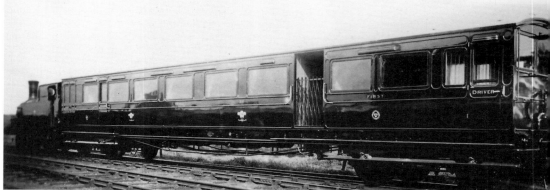

Breach by 349 votes to 70 and admonished by the Speaker.

The case brought improvements for Cambrian staff, who had been working 152hr a fortnight, including a continuous spell of 36hr. However, such arduous rotas stood favourable comparison with those of some companies which made staff work 90hr a week.

Cuts in working hours made it necessary to employ more men and, after World War 1, there was a big increase in locomotive department staff after footplate hours were cut.

Sackings were not confined to hourly-paid workers. Also in the 1890s, William Aston, who had been locomotive superintendent since 1879, was asked to resign after a critical outside consultant's report. He died two years later, leaving as his memorial good locomotives and rolling stock which ran for many more years.

While the Cambrian was slow to recognise trade unions, it studied wage agreements made by bigger companies and in winter 1910 the Midland's general manager, Guy Granet, responded to a Cambrian request for details of a new pay deal for salaried staff clerks.

Staff who dealt with passengers were always well turned-out. Inspectors, passenger guards and ticket examiners wore frock coats and got a small bonus if they kept them smart.

Operating

Staff who drew up timetables faced many problems because of main lines which were not only long but single for much of their length, and often with stiff gradients and sharp curves.

Operating problems were compounded by seasonal traffic variations, with heavy volume during the short 'bucket-and-spade' summer holiday season and by winter storms and gales. Heavy snowfalls were occasionally a problem: in 1886 passengers trapped on a snowbound train near Towyn got out and sheltered with shepherds.

Left:
Locomotives with more enclosed cabs were introduced gradually. Yet 0-6-0T No 13, delivered in 1875 for banking trains over Talerddig, one of the most exposed main line sections, had only a bent-over cab, offering little protection to driver and fireman. *IAL/Bucknall Collection*

Below left:
Passengers were not always as protected from the weather as they may have liked to be. An auto-train built in late Edwardian years had an open, concertina gate dividing the first class compartment (right) from third, through which winds must have howled. Two 2-4-0 tender locomotives were converted into tanks and the coach was formed by two six-wheel coaches placed on a bogie frame. An early example of cost-saving ingenuity. *LGRP*

Above right:
For years the Cambrian Railways was shown as a company in the singular, rather than plural. A commercial postcard got it wrong. Bird Rock was hardly the most striking of the attractions of Towyn, growing slowly into one of the most pleasant and relaxing of the Cardigan Bay resorts.

Passenger services

'A special word of eulogy is due to the Cambrian, whose through trains now vie in equipment with those of the best appointed English lines.' This praise, in a *Baddeley Guide* of 1902, followed the introduction some years earlier of bogie corridor coaches. All had corridors on the up side, to give passengers the best coastal views between Machynlleth and Aberystwyth.

The first passenger service had begun with the opening of the Llanidloes & Newtown Railway in 1859. The initial timetable of three trains each way could not be increased until more coaches arrived the following year. The trains, making 35min journeys through 12 miles of the Severn Valley, ran only on weekdays.

Timetables used as the railways of mid-Wales were built were recast after the main line between Whitchurch and Aberystwyth opened in 1864, three years ahead of the coast line to Pwllheli. When that was completed, through coach services were introduced between Euston and Manchester (London Road) and Aberystwyth and Pwllheli. Journey times must have seemed interminable: it took nearly seven hours to cover the 152 miles from Pwllheli to Whitchurch. (Euston could be reached rather quicker from Pwllheli via Afon Wen and Bangor.)

Passengers travelling from mid-Wales to such distant places for the first time, saw junctions at Crewe and Shrewsbury far bigger than any they had known.

Through-coach expresses formed the backbone of main line passenger services. Whitchurch was the busiest passenger junction, for in addition to Manchester through expresses, Cambrian services connected there with West of England-North West expresses. Often, Cambrian trains suffered long delays because of trains being handed over late by the LNWR — a factor for which the Cambrian got blamed. Delays of several hours were not uncommon. Although arrival and departure times of passenger trains were altered a little through the years, journey times remained constant.

The most important train of the day was shown in Cambrian timetables as the 'London Express' — the 1pm from Aberystwyth, which covered the 61¾ miles to Welshpool in 2½ hr; a journey time cut by 20min by 1908. Beyond Welshpool, Shrewsbury was left an hour later and arrival times at Paddington and Euston were identical at 8.50pm.

The 'London Expresses' were the forerunners of what became the best remembered of all mid-Wales services: the 'Cambrian Coast Express' between Paddington, Aberystwyth and Pwllheli. Yet it never ran in Cambrian days, because it was not named by the GWR until 1927. That was six years after the Cambrian and GWR had begun running restaurant car trains between Paddington, Aberystwyth and Pwllheli, though only on summer season weekdays.

High hopes that Towyn would quickly grow into a holiday resort because of its fine beaches and attractive setting, backclothed by distant mountains, were soon dashed because of an atmosphere of isolation. Golf, shooting and fishing were in abundance but sportsmen and tourists were deterred by long journeys from England, especially as expresses from the Midlands and London turned

into all-station stopping trains when the Cambrian took them over.

Cambrian Sunday services were sparse, usually confined to a single train in each direction on the main, coastal and mid-Wales routes run to meet mail-carrying obligations. Branch line timetables stated prominently that there were no Sunday trains.

The frequency of branch line services varied. Victorian services were mostly mixed trains, the company replying to critics, who had suffered long delays, that coaches were only attached to goods trains for the convenience of the public. The backbone of local passenger services was part-way stopping trains over the main, coast and mid-Wales lines. There were a few workmen's trains, including a Saturday afternoon working between Harlech and Portmadoc.

Refreshment rooms at remote junctions like Moat Lane and major stations like Oswestry were well patronised because passengers often faced long waits for connections. Sometimes they were welcome breaks for meals on long journeys.

Summer tourists often travelled between coast and country. Typical holidaymakers who moved from the coast to the Wye Valley and South Wales faced journeys of about five hours. Leaving Aberystwyth at 12.30pm, they waited at Moat Lane between 2.15pm and 2.45pm before heading south down the Wye Valley, with the 60 miles to Brecon taking another 2½ hr with 15 intermediate stops, St Harmons, Aberedw and Trefeinon being the only request ones.

Cambrian timetables omitted intermediate timings on the Welshpool & Llanfair Light Railway, which it showed as narrow gauge. *Bradshaw's* did

not make the distinction but included timings at Castle Caereinion of 20min after departures from both ends of the line.

Goods and Mineral Traffic

Extra goods and livestock trains ran on local fair days, when local passenger trains were often busy, though overcrowding was rare.

Unlike most other railways, the company's passenger mileages and revenues were far higher than those for goods and merchandise. In 1907 passenger trains ran more than 1,200,000 miles. Goods and mineral workings reached only one third of that total. Six years later, goods and mineral mileage approached 600,000 — about half the passenger mileage. Shunting accounted for well over 300,000 miles.

Annual goods, timber and livestock combined revenues were generally some £30,000-£40,000 less than those for passengers, parcels and mail. Much of the goods and mineral traffic was worked in and out of private sidings, which the Cambrian often helped to finance and maintain. Typical of the co-operation were discussions in winter 1912 with the owners of Tonfanau Quarry which led to the Cambrian repairing and reopening a siding for 'single cargoes' of stone to be sent to Aberdovey Harbour, six miles south. One concentration of private sidings was on the Wrexham & Ellesmere branch, which had five stemming from its 12 miles.

Accidents

The last and worst accident on the Cambrian caused concern throughout Britain about the safety

Left:
Each summer, main line services
were increased to attract
holidaymakers but there were no
alterations to branch line services,
because they ran through country
districts which, however scenic,
attracted few tourists. An auto-
train experiment was carried out
on the Wrexham & Ellesmere
branch shortly before World
Wa 1, partly because it had a
string of closely-spaced stops.
2-4-0T No 56 and its coach were
obviously officially photographed
elsewhere because the single
track branch never threaded hilly
country.
IAL

Above right:
The Abermule disaster of January
1921 had a profound impact on
railway operation, because of
public concern about the safety of
single lines throughout Britain.
The head-on collision was
between an Aberystwyth-
Manchester express and a
stopping train from Whitchurch.
IAL

Centre right:
Abermule wreckage: LNWR
corridor third No 260 in the
foreground. The underframe of
Cambrian composite No 233 is
left centre and between the
coaches is the boiler of the
stopping train engine, 4-4-0
No 82 and above it, the driving
wheels and frame of the express
4-4-0, No 95. *IAL*

Below right:
Such was the tangle of wreckage
that breakdown gangs worked
nonstop for over two days to
clear the scene. The breakdown
train is headed by 0-6-0 No 31.
LCGB

of trains running on single lines. It was the head-on collision between the 10.25am express from Aberystwyth and a local train at Abermule on 26 January 1921. Sixteen people were killed and a man died later. Fourteen passengers were injured. The cause, basically due to failure of the human element, was complex and has been so well documented that the story does not need repeating. In Volume 2 of *The Cambrian Railways*, Bob Miller and I reprinted with thanks the account of L. T. C. Rolt in his book *Red For Danger*. I commend it again. We added a reflection that: 'Things on the Cambrian were never quite the same after Abermule and some of the tarnished safety record was rubbed off on the GWR by critics who feared there might be a repetition of the crash unless the whole line was doubled.'

One other accident made national headlines. The Welshampton disaster of June 1897 caused the first deaths among passengers in the 33-year history of the company. It was particularly poignant because all the 11 fatalities were children. Fifteen passengers were injured, many severely. The train was a Sunday School excursion, carrying about 330 passengers returning from Barmouth to Royton, near Oldham. The heavy train of 15 Cambrian and Lancashire & Yorkshire vehicles was double-headed by Cambrian 0-6-0 tender locomotives Nos 75 and 77 (both built in 1894 and withdrawn by the GWR in 1938). As both stayed on the track, the Cambrian contended that the cause was a rough-riding L&YR brake van, but a Board of Trade Inquiry found that the rails were too lightweight for fast running and many sleepers needed replacing.

The Inspecting 0fficer, Lt-Col H. A. Yorke, stated that some track renewal and remodelling on the system had helped to increase traffic volume but there was a price: 'The company have entered with much spirit into competition for holiday and excursion traffic, and it behoves them to spare no expense in rendering their line strong enough to support the heavy engines and rolling stock now in use, and to endure the wear and tear due to longer and more frequent trains.'

The accident was remembered locally for years and in the 1960s Bob Miller and I called at the village inn in Bettisfield to inspect a broken Cambrian luggage rack mounted in the bar. It was inscribed, 'In memoriam, Cambrian Railways Disaster, 1897'.

Another child tragedy occurred only two months after the Welshampton disaster, when the two-year-old son of a driver was killed by a train at Oswestry. It was noted in *Mishaps on the Cambrian Railways*, published by Elwyn V. Jones, owner of the Severn Press at Newtown, in 1972. Among other accidents briefly detailed was one in winter 1861, when excessive speed was blamed for the crash of a goods train which killed the driver and fireman. The driver was allegedly drunk.

Track renewal work was continuous and as with

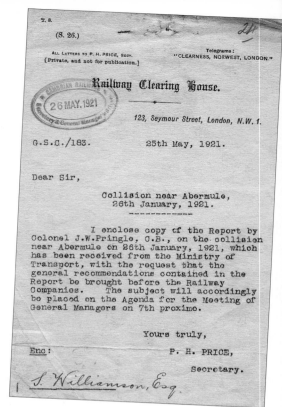

wages, it was policy to consult bigger companies: in 1891, the Manchester, Sheffield & Lincolnshire was asked for technical details of its permanent way. Three years later, tenders were invited for relaying 25 miles of varying lengths of the inland and coast sections in the 'most workmanlike manner'. Baltic wood sleepers and double-headed rails had to be filled in with new ballast and the work completed between May and September.

Fares and tickets

General ticket policy was influenced largely by those of bigger companies, especially those which ran through coach services. Tourist tickets, valid for two months, were issued from the beginning of May to the end of October. A 1904 guide stated that there was 'very little alteration in the fares from year to year'.

An initiative of 1899 was the introduction of 500- and 1,000-mile coupons, but only for first class passengers: nothing similar was offered to second or third class travellers.

For years, the company had an ambivalent attitude towards second class. It abolished it in 1893 but restored it five years later on its main services and on most local lines in 1900. This was because the LNWR and GWR were still carrying second class passengers and wanted through bookings for them. The Cambrian finally abolished second class in 1912.

Left:
The company received the official report into the Abermule disaster in January 1921, only four months after the accident. A copy was addressed to the general manager, S. Williamson. *Author's collection*

Above right:
Victorian guidebooks warned travellers that Friog Rocks, where the Coast line runs on a narrow ledge, 'tends to try weak nerves'. Over the years there have been several spectacular accidents in which railwaymen have been killed. 2-4-0 No 29 *Pegasus* lies wrecked on rocks nearly 90ft below the Coast line, after being hit by a landslide in a storm on New Year's Day 1883. The driver and fireman of the train — the 5.15pm Machynlleth-Barmouth — were both killed. *R. W. Miller*

Centre right:
The crew was also killed by a landslide at Friog in 1933, when the locomotive and tender of the morning mail from Machynlleth were hurled down the cliff face onto the rocks. The locomotive was GWR No 74. As Cambrian No 100 it had been derailed by a landslide at Talerddig in 1921, a few days before the Abermule disaster. *R. W. Miller collection*

Below right:
Excessive speed was blamed for an accident at Nantmawr Junction, when 0-6-0 No 31 was thrown on its side while heading Great Central stock. The driver was sacked and as a precaution, the branch was barred to similar locomotives. *IAL*

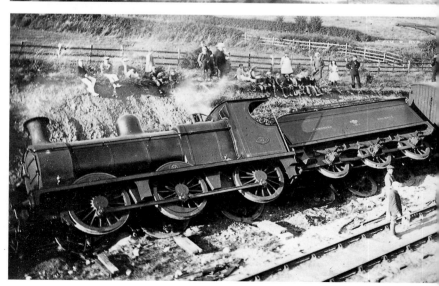

Locomotives, Sheds and Rolling Stocck

Possibly because it was a small company, there was little recognition of Cambrian enterprise in introducing 4-4-0s when the type was unusual in Britain.

Although the locomotive fleet was small — it finally totalled only 99 — it was full of variety and character, dating from the earliest days when engines carried only names. They belonged originally to the contractor Thomas Savin, who built and worked most of the lines. In winter 1863 his motley collections of engines and rolling stock were bought by a Joint Committee controlling three of what became the Cambrian constituent companies: the Llanidloes & Newtown, the Oswestry & Newtown and the Newtown & Machynlleth. The locomotives, and also rolling stock, were then hired to Savin, who went bankrupt in 1866.

The earliest known stock list of October 1861 included seven engines belonging to the Oswestry & Newtown Railway, four of which had been built for the Llanidloes & Newtown. Seven 0-4-2 tender engines forming the 'Volunteer' class were built by Sharp, Stewart in 1859-60. They had 5ft 0in wheels.

Between 1861-3 Sharp, Stewart supplied the O&N with eight 0-6-0 goods engines and began a link with Cambrian-associated companies which lasted for 30 years. In 1863 Sharps supplied two 2-4-0 passenger engines which with the 0-6-0s formed the backbone of the fleet during those three decades. The 0-6-0s, numbered and named, had 4ft 6in wheels and the passenger engines had driving wheels a foot larger in diameter.

In the first year as the Cambrian, the company ordered six 0-6-0 goods engines from Manning, Wardle, builders of several locomotives Savin owned, and six 2-4-0 side tanks from Sharps. Both orders were affected by a financial crisis which followed Savin going bankrupt. The goods engines which had been completed were sold by the makers; two to the London, Brighton & South Coast Railway, the others to the Taff Vale: while only three of the 2-4-0 side tanks were built and delivered. They were the first Cambrian locomotives to have cabs, although rather primitively formed by roofs bent over to cover the bunker. There were no side sheets.

In the early days locomotives were named to give the company a sense of identity with local towns and communities. The net was cast wide: four of the 1859-60 batch were named after the homes of directors, another, *Volunteer*, reflected military presence, the 'honour' here being of the Montgomeryshire Railway Volunteers, a forerunner of the Territorial Army.

Victorian pomp (English rather than Welsh) might explain one of three 0-4-0 saddle tanks built for the minor Porthywaen and Kerry branches in 1863, being named *Prometheus*.

The Cambrian's first fleet of 49 locomotives dated from the company taking over the working of its own line on Savin's failure. But Alexander Walker, officially appointed locomotive superintendent in April 1867, did not have anything like that number to superintend. For the ranks were depleted by 11 which Savin had transferred to work on the Brecon & Merthyr and Hereford, Hay & Brecon Railways, and two others were on small railways in North Wales. Eventually, it was agreed the B&MR could retain five. The rest were returned.

With a single exception, the 1876 stock of 42 engines had been designed and built by Sharp, Stewart. The second largest class, after 0-6-0 goods engines, was formed of 12 'Albion' 2-4-0s working the principal main line passenger trains. Weighing less than 25 tons, they lacked the power to handle increasingly heavy expresses so, in 1878, two 4-4-0s were bought from Sharps to cope with rising summer holiday traffic.

Not only did they bring increased power to the Cambrian, but also gave its locomotive fleet a new look. Among new features were boiler pressures

Above left:
The first locomotive to work on the Llanidloes & Newtown: 0-4-2ST No 3, formerly named *Milford*. A Sharp, Stewart product of 1859, it was photographed at Oswestry after the addition of a rather ungainly cab.
IAL/Bucknall Collection

Left:
No 9, a neatly proportioned 0-4-2 tender engine, originally carried the name *Volunteer* — the title of a class of seven 0-4-2s built by Sharp, Stewart in 1859-60. Several worked on the Llanidloes & Newtown.
IAL/Bucknall Collection

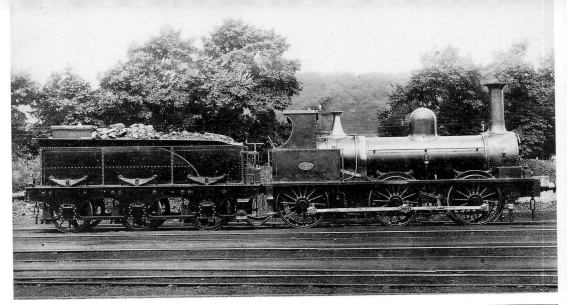

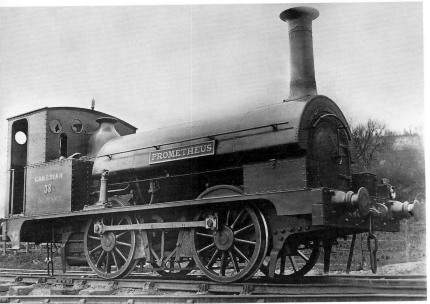

increased to 140psi — 20psi more than that of all previous Cambrian locomotives — full cabs and neat built-up chimneys. There were no locomotive brakes, only handbrakes on six-wheel tenders.

The engines were named after politicians — *Beaconsfield*, the Prime Minister and *Hartington*, the Opposition leader. From about the mid-1880s, names were removed from tender locomotives because the directors felt named engines were ostentatious. But Bob Miller believes there might have been another reason: English staff could not pronounce some names!

Locomotives of the Mid-Wales Railway were taken into Cambrian stock in spring 1888. Originally the MWR had six Kitson 0-4-2 passenger engines and six goods 0-6-0s with the same type of boilers, dating from 1864-5. Most were of little use to the Cambrian. One was quickly sold and another five went to 1898. Only two survived until 1922.

At the turn of the century, the stock was at its neatest and most uniform in appearance, with most of the 83 locomotives bearing a family likeness.

Herbert E. Jones, appointed locomotive superintendent after the sacking of William Aston, had been in office for only two years when the first new engine was built at Oswestry Works — a Class 61 4-4-0. It was constructed so that the company could compare the cost of building locomotives with

that of buying them. It was completed in 1901 and followed by a second of the same class in 1904. Meanwhile, in 1903-4, Jones introduced two classes of tender engines with Belpaire fireboxes, which were a major enlargement of Aston's standard classes. Five goods 0-6-0s were followed by 4-4-0s, all being ordered from Robert Stephenson. The 4-4-0s remained the largest engines to work over the main line until GWR 'Manor' 4-6-0s arrived in 1943.

Faced with financial stringency in 1905, the Cambrian bought five 0-6-0s by instalments, paying Beyer, Peacock £500 as each one completed 1,000 miles of running and meeting the balance by quarterly payments.

A policy of buying secondhand engines, although generally successful, led to the purchase of locomotives of as little use as most of the Mid-Wales Railway stock. It happened when the Cambrian was tempted by six Beyer, Peacock

4-4-0 side tanks, sold cheaply by the Metropolitan Railway in 1905 after electrification. Most were already over 30 years old — as old as locomotives they were meant to replace. High axle loading kept them off branch lines and limited water capacity restricted their main line potential. In 1915, one was converted to a tender engine by Beyer, Peacock and another at Oswestry. The rest were left as tanks because of their poor condition. Today, as failures, they are among the company's best remembered locomotives.

The last locomotives built for the company were five 0-6-0s ordered from Beyer, Peacock in 1915. Because of wartime conditions, the last was not delivered until 1919.

Narrow gauge locomotives of the Welshpool & Llanfair and Vale of Rheidol were among 99 Cambrian engines transferred in 1922 to the GWR, which allocated its own numbers according to wheel arrangement. Although the Cambrian officially ceased to exist from 25 March 1922, it was not until 10 September that they were actually added to GWR stock.

Our David & Charles history details attempts to find new locomotive designs to overcome the handicaps of severe weight restrictions on sharply curved main and branch lines, some laid with light track. Most interesting of projects was for a Mogul for the main lines, designed by the last of the locomotive superintendents, George C. McDonald, who only took office in 1919.

Left:
Three 2-4-0s which formed the 'Seaham' class were the first Cambrian locomotives to have cabs, although they were rather basic and without side sheets. They were built by Sharp, Stewart in 1865-6.
IAL/Bucknall Collection

Below left:
Looking like an ancient warrior, GWR 0-6-0 No 898, originally Cambrian No 14. It was built by Sharp, Stewart in 1875, rebuilt in 1897 and ran for another 50 years. *LPC*

Above right:
'Queen' class 0-6-0 No 51 was among the first locomotives bought by the Cambrian after its formation. It was 57 years old when it was transferred to the GWR at the Grouping and renumbered 910. It was built by Sharp, Stewart in 1865 and survived until 1935. *LPC*

Centre right:
No 74 was the second of five Aston-designed 0-6-0s built by Neilson of Glasgow in 1894-5. It was rebuilt by the GWR soon after Grouping and worked until 1946. *LPC*

Below:
No 77 was the last of the Neilson batch of 0-6-0s. It was rebuilt by the GWR in 1929 and scrapped nine years later. *LPC*

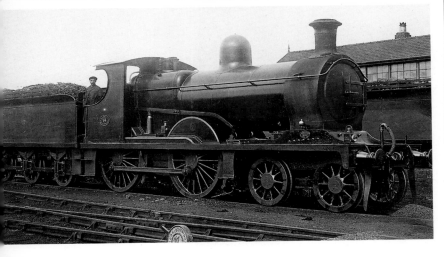

Left:
Another class introduced by Aston was the '3' class of 0-4-4Ts, easily spotted by their unusual rounded porthole-type cabside windows. *LGRP*

Centre left:
No 32, another of the '61' class, was built by Robert Stephenson, Newcastle, in October 1897. As Bob Miller noted in Vol 2 of *The Cambrian Railways*: 'The turn of the century showed locomotive stock at its neatest and most uniform in appearance. Nearly all locomotives had the same family likeness.' By then the locomotive stock had grown to 83. *IAL/Bucknall Collection*

Bottom left:
No 94, the first of five 4-4-0s built by Robert Stephenson at Darlington in 1904, which were the Cambrian's largest locomotives. Axle weight restricted them to the main and coast lines. No 95 was destroyed at Abermule. The last of the five was not withdrawn until 1933. Afterwards, their reputation as the largest locomotives to work over the main line stood until 1942. *IAL/Bucknall Collection*

Above right:
Aston introduced a class of enlarged 4-4-0s with 6ft 0in driving wheels. Designated Class 21, it grew to 21 locomotives built between 1895-1904. No 84 was the fourth and had Scottish origins, being built by Sharp, Stewart, Glasgow, in spring 1895. *LPC*

Right:
Other locomotives restricted in their route availability were six 4-4-0Ts, bought at a bargain price when the Metropolitan Railway was electrified in 1905. No 34 was one of two converted to tender engines. *IAL/Bucknall Collection*

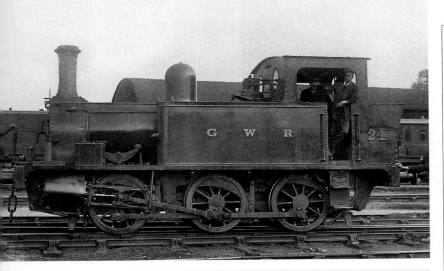

Left:
Perhaps a more useful acquisition by the Cambrian than the Metropolitan tanks, were three 0-6-0 side tanks which formed the entire locomotive stock of the Lambourn Valley Light Railway in Berkshire. The engines, almost new, were sold to the Cambrian for £2,000 — half their original price. The former *Eadwade* is seen as GWR No 24 — its Cambrian number. Later it became GWR No 819 and survived until 1946. *LGRP*

Centre left:
The other rebuild was No 12 — ex-MR No 11. None of the other engines was converted because they were old and in poor condition. Beside No 12 is 4-4-0 No 71, built by Sharp, Stewart in 1894. *IAL/Bucknall Collection*

Below left:
No 44 in its final form as a 2-4-0 passenger tank with rather ungainly 5ft 6in coupled wheels. It was built as a tender locomotive by Sharp, Stewart in 1864, rebuilt for a second time in 1907 and withdrawn in 1923. *IAL/Bucknall Collection*

Above right:
This Beyer, Peacock 0-6-0 carried two Cambrian Nos — 54 and 102 — and became GWR No 896, surviving until 1953. It was a familiar sight on the Mid-Wales route. *IAL/Bucknall Collection*

Right:
No 31, a Beyer, Peacock of 1919, was reboilered by the GWR only five years after building but as GWR No 855 it worked until 1954. *IAL/Bucknall Collection*

Above:
While Grouping and Nationalisation brought an increased variety of locomotives to the Cambrian, *The Earl* and *The Countess*, both 0-6-0Ts, were the only motive power used on the Welshpool & Llanfair Light Railway from opening in 1902 until closure by BR in 1956.
IAL/Bucknall Collection

Below:
Two locomotives built by Davies & Metcalfe of Romiley for the opening of the Vale of Rheidol Light Railway in 1902, a few months ahead of the W&L, were squat and powerful in appearance. Both were 2-6-2Ts. No 1 *Edward VII* is seen in an official photograph.
IAL/Bucknall Collection

Locomotive Sheds

After Grouping, Cambrian sheds formed almost the entire GWR Central Wales Locomotive Division, with headquarters at Oswestry. The only two 'outsiders' were Aberayron — once the Cambrian's Wrexham shed — and the narrow gauge Corris shed. The small Penmaenpool shed was excluded from the Central Wales Division and became a sub-shed of Wrexham Croes Newydd in the Wolverhampton Division.

Oswestry was the largest of the Cambrian sheds, with an allocation of nearly 40 engines. With six roads, it lay between the Whitchurch main line and the Gobowen branch. Despite Whitchurch being only 18 miles from Oswestry, the company kept an engine at its small shed there. *An Historical Survey of Great Western Engine Sheds 1947* by Edward Lyons embraces the history of the Cambrian depots.

Locomotive, Carriage and Wagon Works

On a summer's day in July 1900, soon after he succeeded the sacked William Aston as locomotive superintendent, Herbert E. Jones initialled a large scale plan of Oswestry Works, administered by his department. It had been date-stamped by the engineer's office less than a fortnight before. It seems likely that Jones had it prepared for an in-depth study of the Works, as part of his drive to expand them and install new machinery to meet orders for the building and repair of wagons, including the replacement of dumb buffers with spring-loaded ones.

The Cambrian was without an engineering works when it was formed, but the urgency for them led to the directors ordering specifications to the designs of the Manchester locomotive builders Sharp, Stewart at their first meeting. The board resisted pressure from businessmen at Welshpool to establish the works there because they would be more central to the main line.

More than four million bricks had been laid before Oswestry Works opened in 1866. They won the immediate approval of the environmentally-conscious *Gossiping Guide to Wales*. It argued that while workshops seldom improve the appearance of a place, these added to, rather than detracted from, the beauty of Oswestry. Features included a 150ft chimney — a landmark for miles around — and a tower surmounted by a weathercock which was a fine representation of an 'Albion' class 2-4-0 passenger engine seen broadside. A footbridge to the main entrance spanned nine Cambrian and four GWR lines between the Works and the town.

The Works were comparatively small and while a large number of wagons and carriages were built there, only two locomotives were constructed through the years, although many were extensively rebuilt.

There were other small works: the Cambrian maintained the small Locomotive, Carriage and Wagon Works of the Mid-Wales Railway at Builth from 1888 until closing them in 1903. And because Oswestry was so far from the coast, a small wagon works was opened at Aberdovey in 1880 to reduce the time and cost of sending damaged wagons over Talerddig.

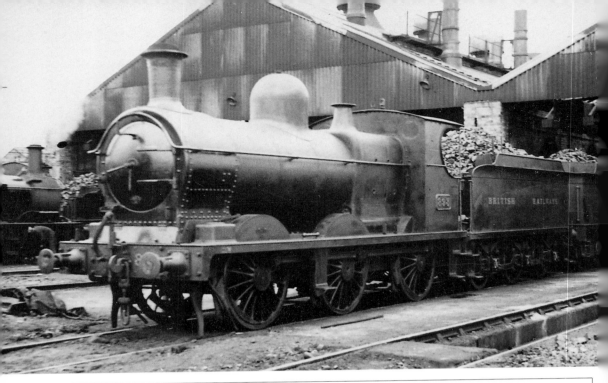

Above:
In its final, rebuilt form, Oswestry shed was more functional; more ugly. Jones Class 89 0-6-0 as GWR No 893 stands with a mountain-stacked tender.
T. J. Saunders

Below:
Three 0-6-0 classes at Pwllheli shed in 1936, GWR No 892 (ex-CR No 930; No 2287 (Collett design) and No 2572 (Dean). *SLS*

Above:
The two road Portmadoc shed was at the north end of the station. BR Standard Class 2 Mogul No 78002was one of four allocated to the Cambrian system in 1963 — the year the shed closed *SLS*

Below:
Portmadoc shed in a busier era — 1936. Outside a trio of Dean Goods, Nos 2323, 2569 and 2449. *SLS*

Above:
Penmaenpool was a sub shed of Wrexhan Croes Newydd in the GWR's Wolverhampton division. The 1936 scene with 0-6-0s Nos 2435 and 2289. *SLS*

Below:
Aberystwyth shed in 1955, two decades after it was rebuilt by the GWR and provided with extra facilities. *SLS*

Above:
The two road, dead ended shed at Llanidloes was one of three Mid-Wales sheds, the others being Builth and Brecon. *SLS*

Below:
Ex LMS 0-6-0 No 3600 was on Brecon shed in 1936 after working over the Hereford, Hay & Brecon route. Also being serviced was Dean Goods No 2342.
W. A. Camwell/SLS

Above:
Brecon variety in 1950. Ex GWR pannier tanks Nos 3706 and 7753 and ex-L&YR Aspinall 0-6-0 No 52414. *SLS*

Below:
A 1953 visit to Brecon found several class on shed including ex-LMS Class 2 Mogul No 46516. *SLS*

Above:
Oswestry lost its status as a railway centre when the
Works closed. The carriage and wagon shops closed in
1964; the locomotive shops in December 1966, by which
time they were the last ex-GWR works to repair steam.
This view shows part of the Works in 1948. *LGRP*

Below:
The wagon paint shop on a summer's day 1907, when the
photographer will have taken advantage of the strong
daylight shining through the roof. Goods brake No 13 is
in the background behind an open wagon.
R. W. Miller collection

Passenger Coaches

Coaches had to be comfortable because of slow timings and long journeys between England and the coast. Early third class coaches were spartan, like those of most companies. When stock was consolidated in 1867, there were 94 coaches. Mostly they were 25ft four-wheelers built in Birmingham by the Metropolitan Carriage & Wagon Co and in Manchester by the Ashbury Railway Wagon & Iron Co. Forty-six were third class; 29 were composites, 16 were second class and only three were exclusively first class.

A number of coaches similar to the original ones were built at Oswestry Works. Luggage was carried in four-wheel passenger brake vans.

Early six-wheel coaches were only three feet longer than four-wheel stock. Oil lamps were withdrawn through coach roofs.

In 1888, the year that Mid-Wales Railway stock was absorbed, the Cambrian had just over 200 vehicles, almost three-quarters being four-wheel coaches dating from 1859-66.

The late Victorian years saw several advances in coach design. Automatic vacuum brakes were introduced in 1886 and in 1893 the company achieved a British 'first' by giving passengers access to the continuous brake. It had been done earlier by the GWR, but only experimentally. The Cambrian introduced bogie coaches from 1895, built at Oswestry and by private contractors. Designs were neat and smart, one feature being turn-under ends to match the contours of the sides. In his Oakwood history, Kidner recalled that at the turn of the century Cambrian coaches made quite a brave showing at Euston, where LNWR stock had long been limited in size by an obsolete carriage traverser.

At this time, Cambrian passengers still lacked two notable amenities: steam heating and restaurant cars. Passengers were 'left in the cold' until their protests led to main line trains being steam heated from winter 1912. Old-fashioned foot warmers (tins filled with hot water and placed under seats) were still found on the branches. This was partly because the company decided to fit steam heating equipment to less than 40 locomotives.

Listed with passenger stock was a variety of four-wheel carriage trucks and vans, passenger brake vans, horseboxes, hound vans and milk vans.

The only restaurant cars on the system were those on through trains operated by other companies. My copy of the GWR summer timetable 1905, with the Cambrian page annotated in pencil by, I presume, a holidaymaker, shows Paddington-Aberystwyth expresses taking over seven hours and carrying a luncheon car only to Shrewsbury. The

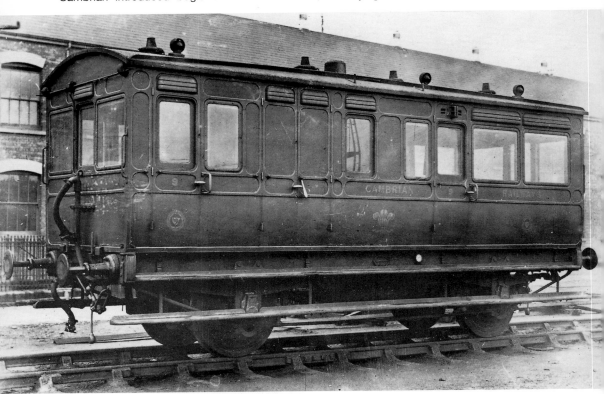

Below left:
An Oswestry product of late Victorian days: first class saloon No 9 of 1889 with double footboards and observation windows at both ends. *Real Photos*

Above:
One of the longest set of Cambrian passenger coaches — brake third No 314 at Oswestry, 1907. The coach was used by passengers who never knew the Cambrian, for it was in GWR and BR stock until 1954.
R. W. Miller collection

Below:
One of only four Cambrian coaches to survive the Abermule disaster: corridor brake composite No 334 of 1909. It was withdrawn in May 1946 as GWR No 6334.
R. W. Miller collection

Cambrian would not have them because it did not want to reduce the custom at busy station refreshment rooms. However, two 'Tea Cars' were introduced. They had a small pantry to serve tea, coffee and light refreshments.

There were also two observation cars, which were attached to the rear of coast trains. They had wooden, throw-over seat backs, to give passengers views out of the rear windows in either direction of travel.

Cambrian smartness was partly due to liveries, basically green with embellishments which changed occasionally. A major change introduced during economies in 1909 was the abolition of white upper panels on coaches, which were afterwards painted bronze green all over.

Goods Rolling Stock

There was little to distinguish the original stock of about 1,000 wagons from that of other companies, apart from brake vans of highly individual design. The earliest open wagons had low sides and dumb buffers. Few had brakes and those that did, had them fitted on one side only. Wagons were bought mainly from private contractors while others were built at Oswestry.

By the mid-1880s, the goods stock had risen to about 1,500. The most common type of wagon grew to be timber trucks.

Three hundred vehicles were added when the Mid-Wales Railway was absorbed in 1888. This was at a time when the Cambrian was short of timber trucks. The addition of 75 from the takeover did not solve the problem, acute because rail was almost the only way of getting heavy timber from large Welsh hill forests to construction sites in Britain's rapidly growing towns and cities.

The Cambrian got its first vacuum-braked goods vehicles — 20 cattle trucks — in 1897. A travelling gas holder ordered in the same year was frequently used on its passenger trains.

Wagon lettering from 1902 was 'CAM * RYS', the asterisk being a representation of the Prince of Wales Feathers. From 1917 the single word, CAMBRIAN, was substituted.

The goods fleet at Grouping of nearly 2,300 vehicles included 1,500 open wagons, nearly 400 timber, rail and flat trucks and almost 200 cattle wagons. It also owned 75 narrow gauge goods vehicles. Many Cambrian vehicles remained in use after Grouping and two goods brake vans were still running in 1959.

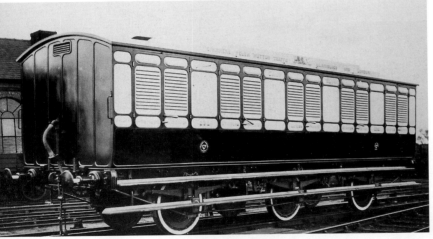

Left:
Six-wheel mutton van No 292 at Oswestry in 1902. The carriage shops also built four-wheel vans for meat and poultry. Vans for other perishable traffic were constructed between 1907-14. *R. W. Miller collection*

Below left:
Eight-ton, low-plank open wagon, built Oswestry 1899. Large lettering and company emblem. The company had more than 1,400 open wagons and nearly 400 to carry rail and timber. *R. W. Miller collection*

Above right:
Goods brake vans were of highly individual design, most having verandas at only one end. Jones-designed van No 10 with Aston tank No 3 of 1895. *LGRP*

Right:
Van No 2 was a 13-ton design. White-painted wheel rims suggest it was photographed on completion in 1902. *R. W. Miller collection*

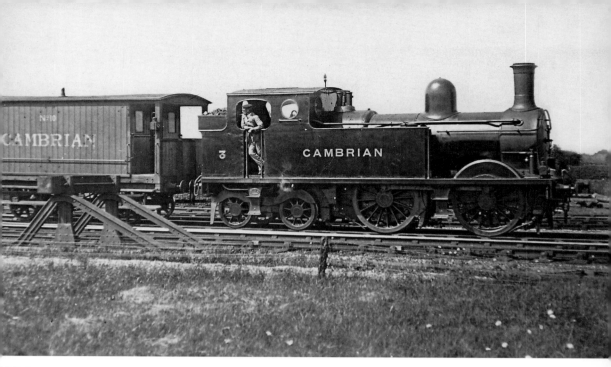

Left:
Kerry station in 1904. This substantial terminus of the 3½-mile line closed to passengers in 1931. *LGRP*

Below:
Welshpool in the summer of 1967 with a Trans-Pennine express DMU forming an excursion from Bradford Exchange to Towyn. The station nameboard was progressively blanked-out as routes closed until only the name of the town remained. *S. Creer*

Stations and Signalboxes

The Cambrian had no stations of striking design, but in the early years they were renowned for their discomfort. Because of low platforms, passengers had to use two footsteps fitted to coaches to climb in and out of them. Many two-platform stations lacked footbridges and passengers walked across the tracks.

Gradually platforms were raised in height and footbridges built, as traffic grew and trains ran faster. Original timber buildings were replaced by more substantial structures of stone or brick, depending on which material was more available locally.

Platforms at most stations were adequate because the longest coaches in Edwardian days were no more than 54ft 6in.

Some stations were far too big. In *Victorian Stations*, Gordon Biddle noted that the Cambrian was bequeathed four remarkably large ones which had been the head offices of constituent companies: Welshpool (1860), Ellesmere and Llanidloes (1864) and Oswestry, built about two years later. Rather smaller were stations built at junctions established in isolated areas where lines joined, rather than near towns, of which there were few in sparsely-populated mid-Wales. Afon Wen, Dovey and Barmouth Junctions were built on the coast and Moat Lane and Buttington, Three Cocks and Talyllyn Junction, inland. Stations were first lit

by oil and later by gas in areas where there was a supply.

Signalboxes and signals were oil-lit. Boxes were mostly small, the largest, Aberystwyth, having no more than 70 levers. There were only five other boxes large enough to be classed as 'A' and busy enough to be manned by double shifts: Oswestry South and Central, Welshpool North, Moat Lane East and Machynlleth East.

Bob Miller, who has made a detailed study of Cambrian signalling, notes that all signals and equipment were bought from private contractors; mainly McKenzie & Holland until 1890, then Dutton & Co, also of Worcester, from 1890-9; J. F. Pease & Co 1899-1901 and finally Tyer & Co of Carlisle until Grouping. By then there were 92 block signalboxes.

Telegraph working on single lines, with instruments housed in station buildings rather than signalboxes, had been introduced well before the Regulation of Railways Act of 1889. At the end of that year, the Cambrian reported that only 45% of passenger lines had points and signals interlocked and was given until April 1892 for completion. But by December 1891 the total had increased to only 68% and the company was granted a further extension of time by the Board of Trade after pleading a special case. The completed proportion reached 97% in 1895 and it is believed that only the Kerry branch remained to be interlocked.

Right:
Aberystwyth station was progressively enlarged after opening by the Aberystwyth & Welsh Coast Railway in 1864. The Manchester & Milford Railway bay platform is to the left. *LGRP/SLS*

Above:
The name of Llyswen, a local village, was added to Boughrod station title in 1912. This mid-1930s scene shows a time when the station had a platform clock, a winter fire in the small waiting room and used old van bodies as storage units. *LGRP*

Centre left:
Brecon (former Brecon & Merthyr) station in 1930. Ex-Cambrian 4-4-0 No 63, heading a local service, was withdrawn later the same year. *SLS*

Below left:
Towyn box controlled a layout, occasionally busy in summer with extra holiday trains, some of which terminated there. *J. Scrace*

Above right:
The Cambrian was a company noted by enthusiasts for the variety of its signalboxes. Talerddig, among the lonely hills, controlled a passing loop of some 700ft, far from being the longest on the system. *J. Scrace*

Right:
A feature of the small Caersws box was its position at the platform end beside a gated crossing. *J. Scrace*

Older signalboxes had separate entrance porches, including Barmouth South (bought by the preserved Llangollen Railway in 1998 for re-erection at Glyndyfrwdy). This was the most common type. Later boxes, built from 1893, were distinguished by a projecting balcony entrance under the main roof. Examples were at Llanidloes and Forden, which still stands. The sole survivor of Tyer boxes is the small one at Castle Caereinion. It dates from 1907.

Signal design varied. Some early McKenzie & Holland versions were surmounted by ornamental finials but the standard Dutton signal, with slightly tapered arms, had only a very plain and almost flat cap to the rectangular wooden post.

Level crossings away from signalboxes, and also opening bridges, were independently protected by signals worked by ground frames but no distants were provided, so the signals were set well back to minimise the danger of over-running.

Left:
Various materials were used in signalbox construction. Harlech was built of brick with a slate roof. *J. Scrace*

Below left:
Criccieth box was another at the platform end, neatly embellished by finials. *LGRP*

Above right:
Service timetables laid down complicated procedures for working at Pwllheli. When necessary, wagons or empty coaches could be propelled in the right direction between East and West signalboxes. West box is seen above. *G. S. Cocks*

Right:
The Cambrian was also noted for some quaint signals. Some had spectacles halfway down the post. An example which survived for years was the Kerry branch distant at Abermule, photographed after Nationalisation. *LGRP*

Far right:
A conventional Cambrian starter was still in use at Llanfyllin at Nationalisation. Most of the company's signals were designed by Dutton of Worcester. *LGRP*

Above:
After Grouping, Cambrian engines worked into new territory. GWR 0-6-0 No 864 — formerly Cambrian No 38 — runs through Saltney with a stopping train bound for the Wrexham line. The fourth coach would appear to be Cambrian. *Real Photos/ R. W. Miller collection*

RAMBLES AROUND the CAMBRIAN COAST

by Hugh. E. Page. 6ᴰ

Left:
The GWR carried on the Cambrian tradition of offering walking tours and rambles. Nearly 300 miles were described in the 1936 guide. It suggested that travellers should not get anything to read on journeys to the coast, as they might miss something better: the fine scenery.

Below:
To keep the home fires burning in the Tanat Valley: 14 tons of household coal sent by the National Coal Board from Sneyd Collieries on the still-described LMS North Stafford Section 12 years after Nationalisation. It was delivered to a wayside station on the GWR Cambrian section.

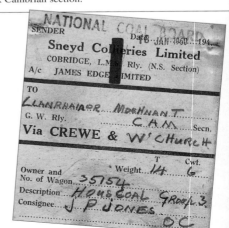

Life After the Cambrian

GWR directors and senior officials who may have thought they were 'swallowing' a small company must have received an unexpected shock when the Cambrian secured the status of a constituent company, a seat on the GWR board of directors and received a guaranteed good income for the 4,000 shareholders.

The shape of the system changed so little that a linen-based system map drawn in the Cambrian Engineer's Office, Oswestry, in January 1920 (possibly in preparation for Grouping) was still accurate at Nationalisation. All that it lacked were the positions of 23 halts, mostly along the coast and

in the expanding Wrexham industrial area, opened between 1923-38.

Three minor branches — the Mawddwy, Kerry and Welshpool & Llanfair — had closed to passengers in winter 1931 and two others had closed completely: the Aberystwyth Harbour branch in 1924 and the Van Railway in 1940.

Although it had never been part of the Cambrian, the GWR placed the narrow gauge Corris Railway under the supervision of the stationmaster at Machynlleth.

Nationalisation and Dr Beeching brought two decades of slaughter to the railways of mid and central Wales in the 1950s and 1960s, leaving the Cambrian system bruised rather than destroyed. It was the GWR secondary route to Barmouth through the Dee Valley, not the Cambrian main line, which closed during the Beeching era. Closure of the 33-mile eastern section of the Cambrian main line between Whitchurch and Welshpool in 1965, and other connecting lines from Carmarthen, Brecon, Bangor and Wrexham, left the Shrewsbury & Welshpool GWR/LNWR Joint line as the only entrance to the Cambrian coast.

Below:
The Oswestry station scene changed little before Nationalisation. A busy winter's morning scene after the arrival of a local service from Gobowen, propelled by a GWR 0-4-2T. It was booked 6min for the 2½mile journey, with an extra 2min allowed if it called at Park Hall Halt. *LGRP*

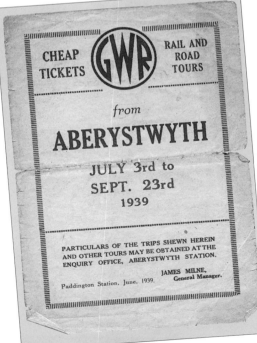

Above:
Smartly turned-out 4-4-0 No 1043 — ex-CR No 98 — is
seen at Swindon with a goods train, having wandered far
on GWR metals. A North Eastern Railway van is next to
the tender. *LGRP*

Left and below:
The outbreak of World War 2 on 3 September 1939 ended
a modest programme of rail and coach tours detailed in a
pocket leaflet. It was issued at Paddington station several
weeks earlier.

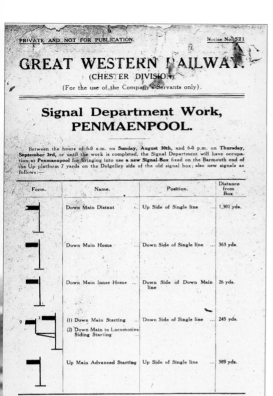

Notice No. 521

GREAT WESTERN RAILWAY.

(CHESTER DIVISION)

(For the use of the Company's Servants only).

Signal Department Work, PENMAENPOOL.

Between the hours of 6·0 a.m. on **Sunday, August 30th**, and 6·0 p.m. on **Thursday, September 3rd**, or until the work is completed, the Signal Department will have occupation at Penmaenpool for bringing into use **a new Signal Box** fixed on the Barmouth end of the Up platform 7 yards on the Dolgelley side of the old signal box; also new signals as follows:—

Form.	Name.	Position.	Distance from Box
	Down Main Distant	Up Side of Single line	1,301 yds.
	Down Main Home	Down Side of Single line	363 yds.
	Down Main Inner Home	Down Side of Down Main line	26 yds.
2	(1) Down Main Starting	Down Side of Single line	245 yds.
	(2) Down Main to Locomotive Siding Starting		
	Up Main Advanced Starting	Up Side of Single line	389 yds.

Above:
Former Cambrian 0-6-0 No 29 finds itself back in Machynlleth shed as GWR No 844 in summer 1953 — about 18 months before being scrapped. The shed was overshadowed by a sheer rock face. *P. B. Whitehouse*

Left:
Replacing the Cambrian Penmaenpool signalbox and signalling layout in August 1936 entailed five days of occupation by the signalling department. The box was telephone-linked to the small engine shed. Instructions were given by the Divisional Superintendent's Office, Chester.

Below:
Viewed from the disused signalbox: desolation at Morfa Mawddach, formerly Barmouth Junction, one of the most scenic of the coastal stations. To the left, the trackbed of the Dolgelley branch, closed in January 1965. *IAL*

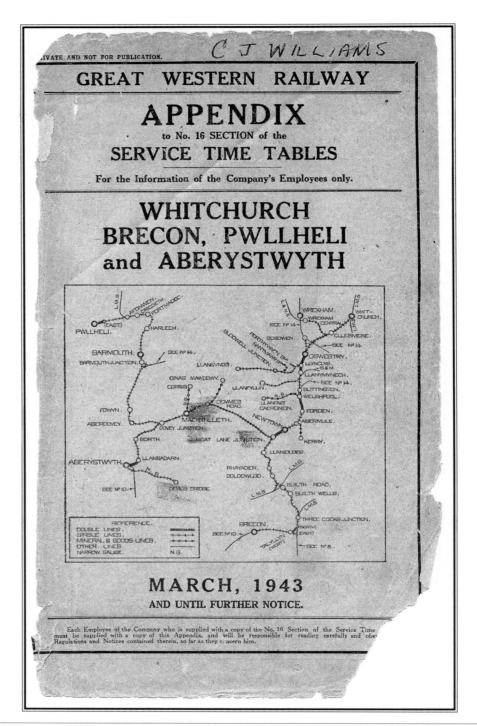

C J WILLIAMS

PRIVATE AND NOT FOR PUBLICATION.

GREAT WESTERN RAILWAY

APPENDIX

to No. 16 SECTION of the

SERVICE TIME TABLES

For the Information of the Company's Employees only.

WHITCHURCH BRECON, PWLLHELI and ABERYSTWYTH

REFERENCE.
DOUBLE LINES.
SINGLE LINES.
MINERAL & GOODS LINES.
OTHER LINES.
NARROW GAUGE.   N.G.

MARCH, 1943

AND UNTIL FURTHER NOTICE.

Each Employee of the Company who is supplied with a copy of the No. 16 Section of the Service Time must be supplied with a copy of this Appendix, and will be responsible for reading carefully and obe Regulations and Notices contained therein, so far as they concern him.

The Cambrian in wartime: a GWR Sectional Appendix of 1943 was issued on the authority of the district traffic manager, Oswestry, Mr T. C. Sellars, once assistant to the Cambrian general manager. After Nationalisation, he was designated district traffic superintendent, Oswestry.

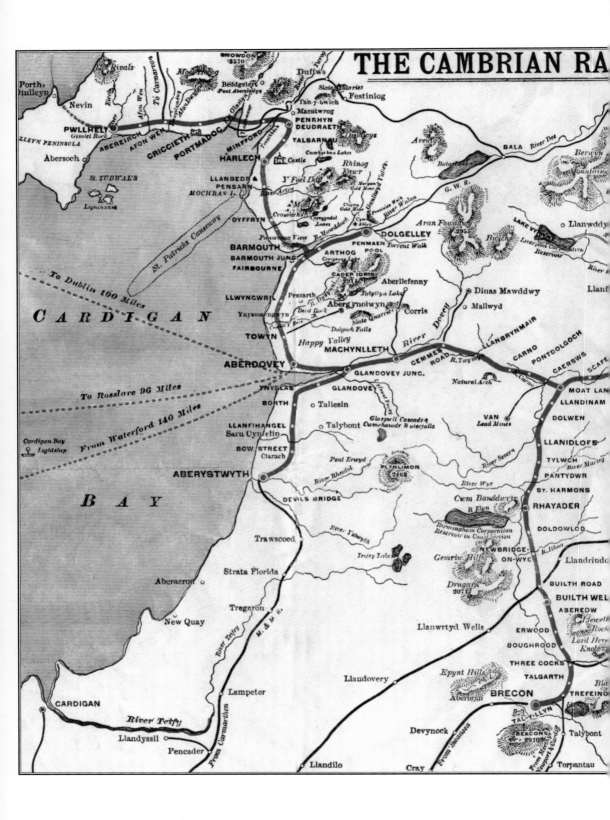